The dual system of vocational education and training in the Federal Republic of Germany

Structure and function

Wolf-Dietrich Greinert

D1702903

 Holland + Josenhans   Best.-Nr. 8010

Published by:
Deutsche Gesellschaft für Technische Zusammenarbeit (GTZ) GmbH
Department "Vocational Training, Technical Education and Human
Resources Development for Trade and Industry"
Eschborn, Federal Republic of Germany

2nd, revised edition 1995

Translated by Joan Tazir and Info-Satz Stuttgart GmbH

© Deutsche Gesellschaft für Technische Zusammenarbeit (GTZ) GmbH, Eschborn

Typesetting: Info-Satz Stuttgart GmbH
Production: Präzis-Druck GmbH, Karlsruhe
Distribution: Holland + Josenhans GmbH & Co., Stuttgart, Federal Republic of Germany
ISBN 3-7782-8010-4

For
Ernst Muche
and
Gerhard Himpel

Foreword

The first edition of this study was published in 1992. The primary motive for writing it was to communicate to foreign experts on vocational training and politicians in this field the complex and singular structure and method of functioning of the German dual system of vocational education and training. For this reason translations into English, French and Spanish followed shortly after the German edition was published, all with the cordial support of the "Deutsche Gesellschaft für Technische Zusammenarbeit (GTZ)" – Technical Cooperation, Federal Republic of Germany.

These texts were distributed primarily within the area of influence of the German vocational training assistance to developing countries, but also widely elsewhere.

The necessity of reprinting the German edition lead to this revision, in which in addition to making necessary corrections and updating the data, chapter 5 has been completely rewritten. With the functional analysis of the dual system which is undertaken here for the first time the author believes that the title of the book is more appropriate than was possible in the first print-run.

I would like to thank GTZ and my publishers Holland + Josenhans for the support they have provided in the attempt to transform what was initially a rather incidental exercise into what in my opinion is now an opus which bears presentation.

Berlin-Friedenau,   Wolf-Dietrich Greinert
January 1995

Table of Contents

Differentiating between the vocational training systems 7

1. The place of learning as a classification criterion 7

2. Basic types of vocational qualifications 10

**The dual system of vocational education and training
in the Federal Republic of Germany**

1. On the historical development of the dual system 23
   1.1 The founding phase of dual vocational training
   (1870-1920) 23
   1.2 The consolidation phase of dual vocational training
   (1920-1970) 26
   1.3 The development phase of the dual vocational training
   system (as from 1970) 31

2. The functional elements of the dual system 37
   2.1 The training market in the Federal Republic of Germany.... 37
   2.2 Vocational Training Legislation in the Federal Republic of
   Germany 46

3. The places of learning in the dual system 57
   3.1 The company as a place of learning 57
   3.2 The industry-wide vocational training establishment as a
   place of learning 63
   3.3 The vocational school as the place of learning 67

4. Vocational training outside the dual system 77
   4.1 The vocational trade schools (Berufsfachschulen)
   in the Federal Republic of Germany 77
   4.2. Vocational further training
   in the Federal Republic of Germany 80

5. Functional analysis of the German training system 87

5.1 Basis of the functional analysis 87

5.2 Making the system functions operational 89
    5.2.1 The qualification function 90
    5.2.2 The allocation function 91
    5.2.3 The selection and status distribution function 91
    5.2.4 The absorption and preservation function 92
    5.2.5 The utilization function 92
    5.2.6 The integration function 93

5.3 Functional analysis of the dual system in the
    Federal Republic of Germany 94
    5.3.1 The qualification function of the dual system of
        vocational training 94
    5.3.2 The allocation function of the dual system of
        vocational training 102
    5.3.3 The selection and status distribution function of
        the dual system of vocational training 111
    5.3.4 The absorption and preservation function
        of the dual system of vocational training 118
    5.3.5 The utilization function of the dual system of
        vocational training 125
    5.3.6 The integration function of the dual system of
        vocational training 133

5.4 The outlook for the dual system of vocational training
    in Germany 138
    5.4.1 An abundance of offers:
        The competing interpretations of the crisis 140
    5.4.2 Expansion of training and missed reforms:
        The real causes of the crisis 144
    5.4.3 The question at the root of training policy:
        Does the dual system of vocational training
        have to be maintained? 150

Differentiating between
the vocational training systems

When posing the question of which vocational training systems are exemplary in international discussions on vocational training nowadays, the German model is one of those on which particular interest is focused. Full-time in-school vocational training of various types as favoured to date is increasingly criticised because of the enormous cost entailed, its distance from practical work and the inherent bureaucracy involved. Integrating (private sector) companies in vocational training is nowadays considered to be an effective approach which the German model fulfils exceptionally well.

However, the discussion on the German dual vocational training system is being influenced by a somewhat distorted viewpoint. The structure of the training system with its places of learning in the company and the vocational training centre is highlighted, while the question of the functioning mechanism of the system is generally ignored. This unsatisfactory perspective results from the method of differentiating vocational training systems according to the place-of-learning criteria, a method that has now became unquestioningly accepted. As the following section will show, such a view confuses the picture rather than clarifies it. The analytical value of such a method is enormously limited due to its lack of semantic precision, the exclusion of the political issue of sponsorship and the static dimension of "place of learning" as a classification category.

1 The place of learning as a classification criterion

In order to indicate the difficulties involved when selecting the place-of-learning criteria, we illustrate below four attempts to identify basic types that we have identified in German literature on vocational training in recent years:

1. Lauterbach[1] arrives at the following classification from his comparison of 12 Federal States: in-company vocational training, in-school vocational training, vocational training in the dual system, mixed systems.

2. Maslankowski[2] differentiates between: the dual system, in-school vocational training, MES training, national vocational training services and on-the-job training.

3. Hegelheimer[3] identifies three basic types from his comparison of seven European countries: dual systems, full-time school systems and mixed vocational training systems.

4. Zedler[4], similar to Hegelheimer, identifies four basic types: the dual system of vocational training, full-time in-school vocational training systems, mixed systems and vocational training in the form of on-the-job training.

It is quite apparent at a first glance that the four classification attempts are not very logical. For example, the MES training specified by Maslankowski is a training method which is used where training systems do not exist. "Mixed systems" as a basic form identified by Lauterbach, Hegelheimer and Zedler is a slip in logic, because it is hardly possible to specify a mixed type as being simultaneously a basic type.

The simple pragmatism behind the four classification systems is very obvious from the fact that most authors do not put forward any classification criteria at all, not to speak of a rationale. Only Lauterbach explains that the question of the place or places of learning plays the decisive role i.e. the aspect of the type of establishment (school, company, workshop etc.) where vocational qualifications are predominantly obtained. Consequently, all four authors uniformly agree in identifying full-time school and company-

1 Lauterbach, U.: (Hrsg.): Berufliche Bildung des Auslands aus der Sicht von Ausbildern, Stuttgart, p. 25 ff.
2 Maslankowski, W.: Das duale System oder welches sonst?, in: Zeitschrift für internationale erziehungs- und sozialwissenschaftliche Forschung 3 (1986), 321-336
3 Hegelheimer, A.: Internationaler Berufsbildungsvergleich. Methodenstudie, Universität Bielefeld 1988
4 Zedler, R.: Standortvorteil: Berufsausbildung, in: Lenske, W. (publ.): Qualified in Germany, Cologne 1988, 75-98

school (= dual) training systems and three authors also indicate the purely company-orientated type (on-the-job training). The national vocational training services indicated as a basic type by Maslankowski do not logically fit into this concept, however. It can, nevertheless, be stated that: the place-of-learning, or the approach based on the aspect of in which establishment vocational training is preferably carried out, has generally become accepted as the criterion for classifying vocational training systems.

While the place-of-learning may be a plausible criterion for classification, it is only of limited analytical value[5]. This is due, on the one hand, to the lacking exactitude of the term[6], and, on the other hand, to its specific use as a (new) pedagogic category. According to the classical definition of the Deutsche Bildungsrat (German Educational Council), places of learning establishments are ''places which differ depending on their pedagogic function. Each place of learning derives its characteristic features from its own functions within the learning process''[7].

An issue which seems to have been consciously excluded[8] is the question of the providing body, i.e. which societal or political power determines the structures and functions of the individual places of learning. The place of learning perspective makes the quasi-unspoken assumption that vocational training systems are primarily generated through pedagogic expediency. A brief overview of the historic genesis of such systems indicates, however, that they are primarily the result of economic and political conflicts of interest, the reflection of power constellations in society. The question of what is most expediently learnt at what place of learning seems to be a very hypothetical question seen from this viewpoint.

---

5   For critique cf. Beck, K.: Zur Kritik des Lernortkonzeptes. Ein Plädoyer für die Verabschiedung einer untauglichen pädagogischen Idee, in: W. Georg (publ.): Schule und Berufsausbildung, Bielefeld 1984, 247-262
6   Cf. Beck, loc. cit. p. 257 ff.
7   Deutscher Bildungsrat. Empfehlungen der Bildungskommission: Zur Neuordnung der Sekundarstufe II. Konzept für eine Verbindung von allgemeinem und beruflichem Lernen, no place of publication indicated, no year of publication indicated (Bonn 1974), p. 69
8   The German Educational Council (Deutscher Bildungsrat) expressly introduced the term ''place of learning'' in the teaching discussion in order to provide a rational basis for the conflict between company and school regarding the optimal location for vocational training processes. Excluding the political dimension of the sponsorship in this way, is quite naive, of course.

9

The place-of-learning as a classification criterion for vocational training systems is, therefore, ruled out just from this aspect alone. Furthermore, it has a static dimension, i.e. although it can be used to describe and analyze institutional structures it cannot describe or analyze the functioning of vocational training. Systems theory in its modern sense must, however, be able to interrelate structure and function[9].

2 Basic types of vocational qualifications

In the attempt to relate the structure and functioning of a social system to each other we are faced with the basic question of which models of regulation determine communication within the system. To put it in concrete terms in relation to our subject: how do we reach the position in which the communicating partners follow certain rules in their system of social behaviour for **Vocational Training** and accept their behaviour in more or less the same model of interpretation? Since the Vocational Training behavioural system is determined by highly divergent social and political interests, it is a question of the **legitimacy** of the behavioural models.

In my opinion we can decipher three fundamental models of regulation in the area of vocational training by reference to **Max Weber**'s sociology of dominion: tradition, market and bureaucratic rationality on a legal basis[10]. **Basic types** of vocational training systems can be assigned to these models of regulation.

Basic type 1: Vocational training is determined by the behaviour provided and legitimatised under common law. Collegially organised private associations decide rules of a nature which form traditions which become the "norm" and place obligations on subsequent providers.

The classic example of the regulation of vocational training via tradition is provided by the **corporate craftsmen's training**, e.g. as was able to maintain its typical structure fairly stably in Germany from the 11th to the 18th century, i.e. for around 800 years. This model of vocational training was and is still very widespread: we find it not only in the history of almost eve-

---

9 Cf. Peschl, M./G. Wunsch: Methoden und Prinzipien der Systemtheorie, Berlin 1972
10 Cf. Weber, M.: Wirtschaft und Gesellschaft, 4th edition, Tübingen 1956

ry country in Europe, but also still today in numerous countries of the Third World.

Tradition means the continuation or preservation of the tried and tested systems which exist. In the case of craftsmen this included both the conditions of vocational training such as vocational practice; i.e. at the core the concept was one of reliable reproduction of the state of the art via an extensive socialisation process. Technical vocational qualifications formed only part of this; traditional vocational training also included general customs, sociopolitical, church/religious and cultural training. The master craftsman had absolute authority over the training [11].

Which traditional regulating mechanisms and instruments characterise the **traditional model** of vocational training?

1. The recruitment pattern of the vocational group is determined by delimitation from outside and maintaining closedness inwards. The most important instrument in this context is strict acceptance conditions for training, which in the end also determine its quantitative dimension.

2. The nature of the technical vocational training is determined by traditional vocational delimitation and the handing down of specific knowledge. Here technical training is only part of an extensive, domestic/familial training process.

3. Regulation and control of vocational training are the responsibility of an autonomous, collegially-oriented corporation, the guild, which draw up binding rules for all the living conditions of the vocational group.

4. As a rule a **teaching fee** must be paid to the master craftsman for the training. If this cannot be paid the training period is lengthened accordingly, i.e. the teaching must then be "worked off".

5. The vocational training process comprises the stages apprentice – journeyman – master craftsman. Only those who have attained the latter level of qualification can provide training and head a craftsmen business.

---

11   Cf. Stratmann, K.: Die gewerbliche Lehrlingserziehung in Deutschland. Volume 1: Berufserziehung in der ständischen Gesellschaft, Frankfurt a.M. 1993

The actual learning model is formed by the imitation principle, the primary points of orientation being the person and the master craftsman's ability[12].

Basic type 2: The vocational training is determined directly by the factor of production "labour" and the qualification signals of the labour market. The form it takes is left on the one hand to the own initiative of individual citizens and on the other to the commitment of (private) operators, intermediaries and other training personnel, who actually offer and run a type of training oriented directly towards application situations undisturbed by government rules.

This type of **market-regulated training system** is found for example in the UK, the USA and Japan. They differ not inconsiderably in terms of structure and their socio-economic conditions of origin, but these countries share the common feature that vocational training is not linked with the general education system, e.g. in the form of vocational schools; neither is there a separately regulated vocational training system guaranteeing a fixed minimum vocational qualification to the majority of the youth. In the countries mentioned there is generally extensive compulsory general school education lasting eleven or twelve years in which the State has a relatively great influence. In principle, all young people attend these high schools and the transition to the tertiary sector is very high in these countries in comparison with the Federal Republic of Germany[13].

On the other hand, vocational training is largely free of government influence. In this market companies naturally play an important role as training

---

12   The model (including for the following functional descriptions) was a corresponding characterisation of the dual system, in our opinion one which is rather to be attributed to the market model, by Ingo Richter; cf. the same: Öffentliche Verantwortung für die berufliche Bildung, Stuttgart 1970, p. 14

13   Cf. Deißinger, Th.: Die englische Berufserziehung im Zeitalter der industriellen Revolution, Würzburg 1992; Nibbrig, B./U. Ziolkowski: Die wirtschaftliche und beruflich-ökonomische Bildung in Großbritannien, Cologne 1982, Münch, J: Berufsbildung und Bildung in den USA: Bedingungen, Strukturen, Entwicklungen und Probleme, Berlin 1989; Lang, D.: Bildung und Berufsausbildung in Japan. Ein Orientierungsmodell für die Bundesrepublik Deutschland?, Konstanz 1984; Georg, W.: Berufliche Bildung des Auslands: Japan. Zum Zusammenhang von Qualifizierung und Beschèftigung in Japan im Vergleich zur Bundesrepublik Deutschland, Baden-Baden 1993

providers. Large companies in particular, because of their economic superiority, achieve a prominent position in the market, as for example in Japan.

What are the mechanisms forming the basis of the functioning of these training systems with the nature of a market? The most important are listed below, though the list does not claim to be exhaustive:

1. The quantitative relationships between demand and training are ascertained via the market model. Vocational qualifications are produced to the extent demanded. The buyers of the qualifications (companies) determine the demand.

2. The nature of vocational qualification (qualitative aspect) is oriented exclusively towards the probable application situations in the companies. Inter-company transfer of the qualifications obtained is variable (depending on the market), but generally low.

3. The mechanism of the market for vocational qualifications works best if the potential buyers of the qualification themselves provide the training and themselves control the results of the training.

4. In this instance the training is financed by the qualification buyer, i.e. it is subject to the principle of cost minimisation. In the normal case it is tied to production and has few pedagogic aspects (on-the-job training).

5. The training provider selects those to be trained without taking into consideration the dominant socio-politically communicated principles, e.g. equal opportunities; the legal position of the trainee does not differ in principle from that of a normal employee.

Basic type 3: Vocational training is regulated solely on the basis of the regulations laid down by the State or by State bureaucracy. In institutional terms, this is a **training system characterised by schools** and is probably the most widespread type of vocational training throughout the regions of the world.

The classic models of school-based vocational training in Europe are found in France, Italy and Sweden[14].

School-based vocational training systems exhibit a high degree of comparability both in respect of their structure and also in respect of the conditions of their origin. They obtain their specific features from the fact that a staged system of vocational schools is closely associated with the general education system; in developed countries, always within the functional area of secondary stage II. Access to the training courses, which are most carefully graded in terms of qualifications, depends on the school leaving results obtained previously at secondary stage I. This link between academic and vocational training is also shown clearly in another peculiarity of this system: the immediate linking of school leaving certificates with (often tariff orientated) vocational qualifications, an element which can be expanded to include the achievement of in effect double-qualification leaving certificates (e.g. university entrance qualification and craftsman qualification).

School vocational training systems are in principle hierarchically organised elite systems, most often found in countries with a strong central administration. Due to this elite position they also generally mark a training monopoly in the area of vocational training, against which competing forms of training (e.g. dual systems) can barely exist [15].

Private companies have no function in these training systems, or only as providers of work experience placements. The greater the claim of the State to sole responsibility in vocational training, the more closed is the bureaucratic system of planning, implementation and control. However, there are examples of the rather indirect interaction of companies in systems of this type: in France, for example, the major chambers of industry maintain vocational schools which are subsidised by the State and they also have to work according to the State training norms.

---

14   Cf. Schriewer, J.: Alternativen in Europa: Frankreich. Lehrlingsausbildung unter dem Anspruch von Theorie und Systematik, in: Enzyklopädie Erziehungswissenschaft, Volume 9: Sekundarstufe II, part 1: Textbook, published by H. Blankertz et al, Stuttgart 1982, pp. 250-285; CEDEFOP (Publisher): Vergleichende Studie über die Finanz-, Rechts- und Organisationsstruktur der Berufsbildung. BRD, Frankreich, Italien, Vereinigtes KÜnigreich, Berlin 1981; ISFOL: Das berufliche Bildungswesen in Italien, published by the Europäische Zentrum für die Förderung der Berufsbildung (CEDEFOP), (Luxemburg 1988); Lauglo, J.: Vocational training: analsysis of policy and modes. Case studies of Sweden, Germany and Japan, Paris 1993
15   Koch, R.: Die Berufsausbildungssysteme in Deutschland und Frankreich, in: Heitmann, W./ W.-D. Greinert (Publisher): Analyseinstrumente in der Berufsbildungszusammenarbeit, Berlin-Schöneberg 1995, 262-272

On the basis of which mechanism do these school systems then function? To list a few:

1. The quantitative relationships between requirement and vocational training are ascertained via State planning bodies. The rationality of such requirements planning functions best if it relates to a limited system of fixed basic vocations.

2. The nature of the vocational qualifications (qualitative aspect) is not oriented primarily towards the immediate vocational application situations but generally takes into account individual and social needs as well. The closer the association between the vocational schools and the general education system and the performance and selection criteria applicable there, the more their technical qualification services are overlaid by and co-defined or redefined by the system problems of the general schools.

3. Planning, organisation and control of the vocational training process are determined bureaucratically to a great extent; implementation of the universalistic principles associated with bureaucratic behaviour tends to guarantee a systematised, highly pedagogic training.

4. School vocational training is financed from public budgets. The limitation of these budgets in principle does not generally allow nationwide training models for the vocational qualification of all of an age group.

5. School models tend to function preferably in vocational areas and vocations in which people can be trained without major psychomotoric skill training, i.e. in commercial vocations, for example.

These basic types of vocational qualification which are controlled by only **one** pattern of regulation are counterpoised by a number of mixed types, some of which are very widespread, which integrate at least **two** regulation patterns.

A combination of market regulation and a greater or lesser degree of State (or bureaucratic) flanking make up what are known as ''cooperative training systems''. In my opinion these may be divided into three tried and tested variants:

15

1. **The model of "formation en alternance"**. These are very often found in countries with traditional **technical secondary schools**, such as France and the areas of its former colonial influence. The knowledge that future-oriented training is difficult to achieve without supplementary in-company qualification phases has often led these countries to make partnership agreements between technical secondary schools and companies or to introduce more extensive systematic periods of work placements. In France, for example, the vocational equivalent of "A" levels ("Baccalauréat Professionel") has taken the form of training which alternates between school and work as a binding principle of the organisation of the training[16].

2. **Industry-wide training model with Latin American features**. This model is defined less by its immediate training organisation than by its form of financing. The companies of an economic sector – industry, trade, agriculture, etc. – are obliged by law to pay a vocational training levy which is proportional to their gross payroll into a central fund, from which the construction of a (national) vocational training organisation which includes central training institutions is financed.

The "national vocational training services" of Latin and Central America are generally facilities in private law whose standard-setting and administrative bodies (= control committees) are occupied by representatives of the employers' organisations, the ministries (education and labour) and also the unions. In industry-wide training workshops, technology centres and mobile training facilities courses for both basic and specialist vocational training, partial qualification and every form of vocational further training are offered. Training and testing guidelines, auxiliary and teaching aids are produced in direct cooperation with the companies according to prescribed methods and procedures [17].

3. The third "cooperative" training model is the so-called **"dual" vocational training system with German characteristics** in which the State lays down more or less extensive framework conditions for vocational training in private companies and other private training providers.We can therefore call this system a State-flanked market model. It occurs only in

---

16 Ditto, p. 269 f.
17 Cf. Arnold, R. et al: Duale Berufsausbildung in Lateinamerika, Baden-Baden 1986; Schleich, B: Förderung der beruflichen Bildung in Lateinamerika, Berlin/Mannheim 1985

German-speaking countries, i.e. apart from the Federal Republic of Germany also in Switzerland and Austria[18]. In these countries there is a marked traditional culture of craftsmanship, which with its corporate vocational education model marks the point of association and starting point of the "dual" vocational training system. The dual system of vocational training in the German cultures arose by means of a State-enacted modernisation act aimed primarily at reorganisation of the craft professions. Laws and bureaucratic forms of regulation replaced the autonomous right of guilds. However, traditional factors can still be seen in the dual training system, e.g. in particular the principle of **vocationally organised labour**.

This system is called dual because two places of learning – the company and (State) vocational school – cooperate with the shared aim of providing the trainees with vocational qualifications. The nature of the duality is however variable; dual systems are conceivable with only one place of learning or with more than two places of learning.

One aspect characteristic of dual models of vocational training is the relatively sharp delimitation of a vocational training system as against the general public school system. This delimitation is visible above all in the existence of more or less extensive specific vocational training legislation which cannot be assigned to the category of school legislation. The legal responsibility for vocational training in such systems therefore tends to resort to the economic or labour authority.

The dual system can be defined as a "vocational-pedagogic structure" (Münch), i.e. a learning system with two places of learning, only in respect of its institutional character; its functional duality, on the other hand, is based on the integration of two different patterns of regulation with a view to vocational training. An inevitable precondition is that there must be a training sector structured according to the rules of the private economy (i.e. the rules of the market) which the State can then shape by means of legal standards. This integration is reflected most clearly in vocational training legislation, i.e. also for example in the Vocational Training Act of the Fed-

---

18 Cf. Greinert, W.-D.: The "German System" of Vocational Education. History, Organization, Prospects, Baden-Baden 1994, deutsch: 1993; Schermaier, J.: Die Formen der gewerblichen Berufserziehung bis zum Facharbeiterniveau in Österreich. Unter besonderer Berücksichtigung des Duo-Systems, Vienna 1970; Wettstein, E./R. Bossy et al: Die Berufsbildung der Schweiz. Eine Einführung, Luzern 1985

eral Republic of Germany of 1969 (VTA), in which the private sector of the market is purposefully embraced by the public sector [19].

What functional criteria can be derived from this basic pattern? The following are undoubtedly important:

1. The quantitative relationship between need and vocational training is certainly determined by the market (seller's market!); however, if the companies offer training they are subject to the State standards set.

2. The nature of the vocational qualifications (qualitative aspect) is oriented primarily towards vocational application situations at work. However, as well as the companies, the State and interest groups (e.g. unions, professional associations) also affect the definition of qualification aims.

3. The companies are providers of training. The vocational training processes must however be organised according to State-specified standards and are subject to direct or indirect State control.

4. The costs of the training are borne principally by the companies. It is characteristic of dual training models that they have regimented financing models[20] (e.g. fund financing) and/or a greater or lesser degree of subsidization by the State, as for example the financing of the vocational schools in the Federal Republic of Germany.

5. The degree of systematisation of vocational training and the degree of pedagogics in dual training systems can be determined in principle according to need. The greatest lever for such control is offered by variation of financing modalities.

We must not make the mistake here of misunderstanding the types of formalised vocational training which we have developed as direct copies of real forms of national vocational training systems. All the existing vocational training systems in the various countries are rather by our understanding variants and/or combinations of the three basic forms or of basic forms with mixed types. The types which we have developed are therefore

---

19 Cf. e.g. Götz, H.: Berufsbildungsrecht. Eine systematische Darstellung des Rechts der Berufsausbildung, der beruflichen Fortbildung und der Umschulung, Munich 1992
20 Cf. e.g. Hegelheimer, A.: Finanzierung der beruflichen Ausbildung, (= Schriften der Deutschen Stiftung für internationale Entwicklung), Mannheim 1986

18

of model character ; there is probably no country in which a type exists in its pure form (so to speak) as a solitary training system.

As with all developed vocational training systems, that of the Federal Republic of Germany is also a complex combination of special types of training. One form of organisation is however dominant, and that is the dual system with its core of a vocationally structured training scheme [21].

The organisation of industrial labour and training in the Federal Republic of Germany is thus essentially characterised by a specifically German type of labour, i.e. "skilled worker" or the specialist workforce, who have obtained their qualifications and their vocational knowledge through vocational training standardised by the State within the framework of the "dual system" of company experience and vocational school. Specialist work, as a vocational pattern of training and labour, has left a decisive mark on the recruitment and employment policy of German companies and largely defines the exchange processes in the labour market and is at the same time a point of reference for State and union social and labour policy.

This typical networking of the training sector with the employment system which is based on a long tradition makes it seem problematic to recommend to other countries – preferably developing countries – that they adopt the dual training system in an undifferentiated manner. With such "system consultancy", which operates with apparently neutral references to the functional reliability of isolated institutional arrangements for vocational training, the essential determining factors of vocational training systems are blotted out: the historical and cultural conditions of origin of such arrangements, but also their integration in previous and subsequent bodies such as familial socialisation, the general school system, social value judgements, etc. Above all, however, the dependence of vocational training organisation on the specific recruitment, employment and labour organisation conditions of the companies in a national economy are not taken into consideration[22]. The attempts started to date at implementing dual training

21 Cf. Greinert, Das "deutsche System". – loc. cit., p. 117 ff
22 Cf. Georg, W.: Zwischen Markt und Bürokratie: Berufsbildungsmuster in Japan und Deutschland, in: the same/U. Sattel (Publisher): Von Japan lernen? Aspekte von Bildung und Beschäftigung in Japan, Weinheim 1992, 42-69, p. 44 f.

structures in other industrial or developing countries cannot provide a basis for optimism concerning the opportunities for transfer of the dual system[23].

Our analysis, which takes into account the structure and functional mechanisms of the dual system to equal degrees, should help to shed light on its complexity and guard those responsible against making premature recommendations and decisions. The following account was concluded in July 1990 and revised in 1994. It deals almost exclusively with the situation in the former West Germany (the "old" Federal states). It will probably be a few years before it is possible to describe the situation throughout Germany as the "normal situation". In order to be able to clarify the current overall extent of the dual system in Germany, where possible recourse has been made to new data on vocational training in the former East Germany (the "new" Federal states); however, this does not mean that the picture of the situation of vocational training throughout Germany is entirely complete.

---

23   Cf. e.g. Schmidt, H./H. Benner: Das duale System der Berufsausbildung – Ein Export-schlager? – Möglichkeiten und Grenzen der Übertragung eines Berufsbildungssystems, in: Arnold, R./A. Lipsmeier (Publisher): Betriebspädagogik in nationaler und internationaler Perspektive, Baden-Baden 1989, S. 341-353

The dual system of vocational eduction and training in the Federal Republic of Germany

An adequate description of the vocational training system in the Federal Republic of Germany, which gives an insight into its functioning, cannot be provided by simply explaining its core area, the dual system and its institutions; at least three other areas must also be dealt with.

1. The historical dimension of vocational training in Germany. As vocational training in the Federal Republic of Germany is not the product of a set, planned structure but rather is a product which has slowly developed on the basis of socio-economic and vocational training traditions, it is important to understand the major lines along which this training system developed.

The decisive role of the historical component when appraising the "dual system" is illustrated simply by the fact that it was not termed as such until the 1960s[1] (and can only be termed a "system", i.e. planned, structured overall vocational training, in the Federal Republic of Germany since the adoption of the Vocational Training Act (VTA) of 1969). The second German nation that was founded following the war and existed up until 1989, the German Democratic Republic, took a different path, which in their opinion and indeed which objectively lead to the "defeat" of the dual system of vocational training[2]; in our typology their system became a bureaucratic system.

---

1 The term is used for the first time in the „Gutachten über das berufliche Ausbildungs- und Schulwesen" (1964) of the committee „Deutscher Ausschuß für das Erziehungs- und Bildungswesen"; it probably originates from Heinrich Abel (1908 - 1965), Professor for Vocational Education Theory of the Technical University Darmstadt and member of the committee.

2 Cf. Biermann, H.: Berufsausbildung in der Deutschen Demokratischen Republik. Zwischen Ausbildung und Auslese, Opladen 1990, S.6

2. Vocational training outside the dual system. As mentioned in the introductory chapter, the Federal Republic of Germany's vocational training system is a complicated combination of the three basic types of vocational training which developed in this country. The dual form of organisation, however, predominates absolutely. Around 75% of 16-19 year olds receive their vocational training in the company with concomitant attendance at vocational schools. In-school vocational training in the Federal Republic of Germany is particularly widespread in trades involved in health and the social services and in the commercial and domestic science sectors. On the other hand, basic vocational training provided in schools, which has been growing in importance since the 1970s, is a component part of the dual system.

The market model is characteristic for the vocational further training sector in the Federal Republic of Germany: its chief features are that it is independent of state regulations, it provides a heterogeneous, extremely application-oriented (job-oriented) training, participation is voluntary and all variations of mixed financing are possible.

Nowadays, this further training system in particular is the crucial supplement to the dual system. Influential interest groups have, therefore, been attempting for many years now to incite the legislator also to organise vocational further-training upgrading on "dual" lines, or at least to gear it formally to the dual system of initial training.

3. The relationship of the vocational training system with the overall social system, and in particular with relevant subsystems such as the general training system and the employment sector. The relationships of the system with itself are also of analytical interest.

We will attempt to present this part of our account in the form of what is known as a *functional analysis*. It comprises firstly a definition of the problems which the vocational training system must solve for the world around it, and secondly an empirically-oriented determination of the effective problem-solving capacity of the system, i.e. ascertaining its functionality.

1 On the historical development of the dual system

Literature on vocational training widely indicates that the dual system of vocational training in the Federal Republic of Germany originated around the turn of the century[3]. This is only correct to the extent that the elements of dual vocational training became structured around the year 1900: however, no system character was visible at all. We, therefore, typify this first development phase of German development training system as:

1.1 The founding phase of dual vocational training (1870-1920): Restoration of craftmanship training and the further education school

Vocational training organised on a dual basis was created during the said period less because of the need for technical qualifications in a developing industrial nation but rather as a concomitant symptom of a wider political reaction to the social and economic consequences of the dissolution of the bourgeois society[4]. This is the only possible explanation why, on the threshold of the 20th century, Germany passed legislation on manual trades that revived the antiquated training model of manual craftsmen's trades, making it the model for its non-academic vocational training – although this was not foreseeable[5]. The restoration of training in craft trades, derived from training in the Middle Ages with its qualification levels of apprentice – journeyman - master craftsman, took place in the course of the so-called ''middle class policy'' of the Empire; this wide-scale attempt to protect the old middle class which was in a state of social and economic decay (craftsmen, small merchants, small farmers) from proletisation and to transform it into a ''bastion against social democracy''[6].

---

3   Cf. for example, Lipsmeier, A.: Organisation und Lernorte der Berufsausbildung, Munich 1978, p. 103
4   Cf. Obendiek, H.: Arbeiterjugend und Fortbildungsschule im Kaiserreich, Alsbach 1988; Stratmann, K.: Zeit der Gärung und Zersetzung''. Arbeiterjugend im Kaiserreich zwischen Schule und Beruf, Weinheim 1992
5   Cf. Stütz, G. (Publisher): Das Handwerk als Leitbild der deutschen Berufserziehung, Göttingen 1969
6   Cf. Greinert W.-D., Schule als Instrument sozialer Kontrolle und Objekt privater Interessen. Der Beitrag der Berufsschule zur politischen Erziehung der Unterschichten, Hanover 1975

This meant in concrete terms that between 1878 and 1897, and then again in 1908, the majority vote in the German Reichstag, consisting of Conservatives, Centre and parts of the National Liberals, passed some amendment bills to protect retail trades and also a number of amendments to manual trade laws which, while they did not completely fulfil the demands of middle class interest groups, did legalise clear privileges for manual trades and retail trades in the economic sector at the expense of others – in particular the consumers. The major amendment, the so-called "Craftmens' Protection Bill" (Handwerkerschutzgesetz) of 1897, permitted the establishment of chambers of craft as corporations under public law, allowing independent craftsmen to protect their common interests and created the institution of so-called "facultative compulsory guilds" with the aim of limiting competition[7].

While the "major eligibility certificate" (Großer Befähigungsnachweis) which required a master craftsman's certificate in order to exercise a craft trade, was passed by the Reichstag in 1890, this did not pass the veto of the Federal Council (Bundesrat). Instead, a so-called "minor eligibility certificate" was then passed as a somewhat inadequate replacement, and from then on only a certified master was entitled to train apprentices. The 1897 amendment to manual trade laws was not just the most important law passed in the Empire regarding the economic stabilization and reform of manual trades: together with the 1908 amendment, it also became the basis of vocational training in Germany – of the dual system. The amendment completely reformed apprenticeship: paragraphs 126 to 128 contained "general" regulations and paragraphs 129 to 132 "special" regulations i.e. referring exclusively to apprentice training in craft trades; these stipulations anchored a long-lasting privilege for craft trades regarding – quantitatively significant – vocational training[8].

If the revival of manual vocational training can be termed a conservative-clerical variant of the middle class policy, then the attempt to establish the second "pillar" of dual vocational training – the further training school – must be classified as a liberal variant of this policy. Since the 18th century,

---

7   Rinneberg, K.J.: Das betriebliche Ausbildungswesen in der Zeit der industriellen Umgestaltung Deutschlands, Cologne/Vienna 1985
8   Cf. Schlüter, A./K. Stratmann (Publisher): Quellen und Dokumente zur betrieblichen Berufsbildung 1869 – 1918, Cologne/Vienna 1985

these "further training" schools have existed in Germany both as general educational establishments for the youth which have left primary school (Sunday school) and as trade schools – particularly serving the craft trades. But they were neither successful nor effective and their existence was continually under threat[9].

The further training school policy did not take on any greater dynamism until the last third of the 19th century, when as a result of the rapid growth in the population, the gap in secondary socialisation – above all of male youth – became a mass problem for the bourgeois society which could no longer be ignored. However, the first attempt at exercising an educational influence on the youth in employment through a general further training school (adapted to the programme of the people's schools or *Volkschulen*) was a failure[10].

The critical arguments concerning this unsuccessful attempt which began to be heard around 1890 then peaked around 1900 in the proposal made by Georg Kerschensteiner to transform this school into an institution consistently oriented towards the vocation of the pupil and thus to settle on the official middle class policy. Kerschensteiner's idea of integrating the proletariat and lower middle class youth into the national bourgeois state through vocational training or vocations may be understood not only as the central trigger in the direction of vocational schools but also marks – in a de-idealised and international perspective - the "German philosophy of vocational education" to date, as distinct from the widespread models of simple job training.

Between 1895 and 1914 the school reformers centred around Oskar W. Pache and Georg Kerschensteiner and the state bureaucracy – all exponents of bourgeois liberalism – succeeded in expanding the number of vocationally oriented further education schools considerably and to implement these as uniform, compulsory schools supplementing the new order of manual crafts training[11]. The close linking of these schools with a corporate understanding of vocation able to thrive in the lee of a policy promoting middle class and the duty to provide a conservative "citizen's training",

---

9   Cf. Thyssen, S.: Die Berufsschule in Idee und Gestaltung, Essen 1954
10   Cf. Greinert, Schule als Instrument ..., loc. cit., p. 21 ff.
11   Cf. Harney, K.: Die preußische Fortbildungsschule, Weinheim/Basel 1980

25

however, considerably modified this liberal modernisation of vocational training[12]. Here the ''role model of middle-class vocational identity and basic patriotic attitude'' (Harney) which the Liberals and the government had favoured at least since the nineties as a general education model for the clientele of the further education schools was supplemented with advanced elements which allowed this school to become the second pillar of the ''dual system'' of vocational training[13].

1.2 The consolidation phase of dual vocational training (1920-1970): Industry-typical apprentice training and the vocational school (Berufsschule)

The second development phase of dual vocational training is moulded by the attempt to give more modern and clear structures to the training sector, which was still characterized by pre-industrial structures and largely non-uniform training consisting of a rather unrelated mixture of in-company and in-school qualifications. The efforts to this end were uniform in character over practically three political eras: beginning in the 1920s (Weimar Republic)[14], they were intensified in the Nazi era – although linked to specific ideological concepts[15] (1933-1945) and were taken up again in the Federal Republic of Germany, following the collapse at the end of the war – this time being stripped of all ideological concepts[16].

In this politically active development phase three main training-policy chains of activity can be pinpointed:

– the attempt by industry to construct its own modern vocational training model oriented towards rational criteria for its own needs, at the sole discretion of the entrepreneurs;

---

12 Cf. Geißler, Kh. et al (Publisher): Von der staatsbürgerlichen Erziehung zur politischen Bildung, Berlin/Bonn 1992
13 Cf. Bruchhäuser, H.-D./A. Lipsmeier (Publisher): Quellen und Dokumente zur schulischen Berufsbildung 1869 – 1918, Cologne/Vienna 1985
14 Cf. Muth, W.: Berufsausbildung in der Weimarer Republik, Wiesbaden/Stuttgart 1985
15 Cf. Wolsing, T.: Untersuchungen zur Berufsausbildung im Dritten Reich, Kastellaun 1977
16 Cf. Stratmann, K./M. Schlösser: Das duale System der Berufsausbildung. Eine historische Analyse seiner Reformdebatten, Frankfurt a.M. 1990

- the attempt by companies, vocational school teachers and state bureaucracy to create a depoliticised vocational school which as a "lower technical college" was oriented towards the qualification requirements of "the private sector";

- the attempt primarily by union-oriented forces to influence vocational training via a comprehensive law stipulating in particular the rights of participation of those representing the social interests of the workforce.

The problem areas, which had changed from those of the first epoch, which may be considered triggers and driving forces of these political actions, are easy to find: they are the qualification requirements of industry, the loss of the political basis of legitimation for the further training school and the unilateral privilege given to entrepreneurs in respect of vocational training through industrial legislation.

Even in the last phase of the economic cycle prior to the First World War (1895-1913) the qualification requirements of industry had changed as a result of accelerated growth. In the pioneering enterprises in the fields of mechanical and electrical engineering in particular the new orders of magnitude demanded new methods of production along the lines of those developed in the USA[17]. These included specialisation of the production range, detailed prime cost calculation for the individual stages of fabrication, performance targets and checks, the standardisation of replaceable parts and ensuring these through so-called tolerance gauges ("fits").

This thrust towards rationalisation required a new type of industrial worker who, in contrast to the "artistic craftsman" was prepared to subject himself to the requirements and forces of the new production methods. The new training model, which the industry developed from around the mid 1920s, was therefore heavily influenced by the ideas of "Scientific Management" and essentially encompassed three new dimensions: an institutional dimension with a training workshop[18] and a vocational (works) school[19], a methodical dimension of a psychological selection procedure, standardised

---

17 Cf. Hanf, G.: Berufsausbildung in Berliner Großbetrieben (1900-1929), in: Greinert, W.-D. et al (Publisher): Berufsausbildung und Industrie, Berlin/Bonn 1987, 157 – 1987
18 Cf. Behr, M. v.: Die Entstehung der industriellen Lehrwerkstatt, Frankfurt a.M. 1981
19 Cf. Fenger, H.: Die betriebseigenen Berufsschulen industrieller Betriebe in der Bundesrepublik, Diss. Cologne 1968

training courses[20] and teaching aids and a vocational systematic dimension with the "organisational means" of a vocation description, training plan and testing requirements[21]. Special institutions such as the German Commission on Technical Schooling (Deutscher Ausschuß für Technisches Schulwesen or DATSCH), German Institute of Technical Work Training (Deutsches Institut für Technische Arbeitsschulung or DINTA) and the Working Committee on Vocational Training (Arbeitsausschuß für Berufsausbildung) were founded and introduced a systematisation and perfecting of vocational training previously unknown in the traditional craftsman's training[22]. The dominant position of the craft trades in this area was then largely removed through the break-up of its facultative examination monopoly in 1936. With the introduction of the "Facharbeiter" or specialist worker a new type of qualification existed which later, at least since the 1930s, became a leading part of the dual system[23].

Despite this, industry did not succeed in implementing a fully independent vocational training model. In the 1920s, still on a course of confrontation with its "works school movement" and in the shadow of the economic crisis, its specialist worker training was integrated into the organisational framework of the (traditional) dual vocational training with the recognition of the public vocational school (Berufsschule) as the second place of learning[24].

In contrast to industrial training, the further training school, known since around 1920 as the *vocational school*, developed only slowly and unsteadily in this second phase into a generally recognised place of learning[25]. In the Weimar Republic, despite all the demonstrative programmatic state-

---

20 Cf. Wiemann, G.: Der "Grundlehrgang Metall" als systemstiftendes didaktisches Modell einer industrieorientierten Berufsausbildung — eine berufspädagogische Bewertung in: Arnold, R./A. Lipsmeier (Publisher): Betriebspädagogik in nationaler und internationaler Perspektive, Baden-Baden 1989, 179-196.
21 Cf. Benner, H.: Arbeiten zur Ordnung der Berufsbildung vom DATSCH bis zum BiBB, in: Greinert, W.-D. et al (Publisher): Berufsausbildung und Industrie, Berlin/Bonn 1987, 169-293
22 Cf. Pätzold, G. (Publisher): Quellen und Dokumente zur betrieblichen Berufsbildung 1918 – 1945, Cologne/Vienna 1981
23 Cf. Ebert, R.: Zur Entstehung der Kategorie Facharbeiter als Problem der Erziehungswissenschaft, Bielefeld 1984
24 Cf. Hoffmann, E.: Zur Geschichte der Berufsausbildung in Deutschland, Bielefeld 1962
25 Cf. Kümmel, K. (Publisher): Quellen und Dokumente zur schulischen Berufsbildung 1918-1945, Cologne/Vienna 1981

28

ments, it was sidelined in school policy as an instrument for regulation of the labour market and maintaining the work ethic of the young unemployed, particularly during what became known as the stabilisation crisis (1923-1926) and the world economic crisis (1930-1933). All interested parties agreed that the "new vocational school" should primarily be obliged to *promote the ability to exercise a vocation*; however, the periodically increasing number of young unemployed persons of an age at which vocational school was compulsory forced the bureaucracy to use the school primarily as a social catchment device. This socio-political instrumentalisation threatened to destroy the pedagogic-didactic concept of the school, the *idea of the vocation principle*, and thus also its material basis[26].

The basis for standardizing the very fragmented public vocational schooling system was not created until after the Weimar Republic, when the school administrations of the individual states was centralized in a "Reich Ministry for Science, Education and Public Education" (Reichsministerium für Wissenschaft, Erziehung und Volksbildung) in 1934 – although this also created the basis for ideological control by the National Socialists[27]. In 1937 the vocational schools were given standardized names; in 1938 attendance at a vocational school became compulsory country-wide, while in 1940 the time-input for training at vocational schools was stipulated by decree. As from 1937, the central bureaucracy also began to organise in-company training and school instruction more strictly by creating joint, standardised curricula (Reich curricula); in the same year standardised regulations were established on the important issues of sponsorship of vocational schools and their funding[28].

By the end of the 1930s, therefore, the centralistic policy of the National Socialists had thus legally regulated the form of the classical compulsory vocational school: 3-year compulsory vocational instruction, 8 lessons per week, compulsory sponsorship (town and rural municipalities), standardised curricula, vocational schooling closely geared to the in-company training, vocational school counsellors, vocational school teachers held civil

---

26 Cf. Schütte, F.: Berufserziehung zwischen Revolution und Nationalsozialismus, Weinheim/ Basel 1977

27 Cf. Seubert, R.: Berufserziehung und Nationalsozialismus, Weinheim/Basel 1977

28 Cf. Kipp, M.: "Perfektionierung" der industriellen Berufsausbildung im Dritten Reich, in: Greinert, W.-D. et al (Publisher): Berufsausbildung und Industrie, Berlin/Bonn 1987, 213-266

servant status. However, the National Socialist's administration of the training system was not able to ensure that this type of school became implemented in practice – partly because of a lack of time and money, and partly because of a lack of interest. A broadly-based, state-run vocational school system could not be established until after the war, in the Federal Republic of Germany – although it largely followed the legal structure set up in the thirties[29] but was given a federalistic character.

The integration of vocational training legislation into trade legislation, reinforced by the amendments to trade legislation of 1897 and 1908, was questioned at an early date, but it was not until 1919 when trade unions became recognised negotiating partners that an actual political attempt was made to pass a comprehensive regulation on apprenticeship training in a specific act, and also to obtain a right of participation for the trade unions in implementing vocational training[30]. It took 10 years, however, for the Reich government to transmit a corresponding draft law to the Reich parliament; the final consultations and enactment of this law could not take place because of the turbulence due the world economic crisis. Even the National Socialists did not succeed in enacting their frequently drafted legislation, primarily due to the massive struggles for influence in vocational training between the German Labour Front (Deutsche Arbeitsfront = DAF) and the Reich ministry of economics.

After the war, efforts to establish a specific and uniform legislation for apprenticeship training continued, although it was not until 1953 that the craft trades were able to establish comprehensive vocational training regulations within the scope of the ''Trades Regulation Act'' (Handwerksordnung). Discussions recommenced in 1959 on the initiative of the trade unions, but the two large political parties, the Social Democrat Party (SPD) and the Christian Democratic Union/Christian Socialist Union (CDU/CSU), did not agree on a joint legislative initiative until the end of the sixties – resulting then in the adoption of the Vocational Training Act (Berufsbildungsgesetz -BBiG) on 14th August 1969[31]. Although it only became apparent

---

29 Cf. Grüner, G. (Publisher): Quellen und Dokumente zur schulischen Berufsausbildung 1945-1982, 2 vol., Cologne/Vienna 1983

30 Cf. Pätzold. G. (Publisher): Quellen und Dokumente zur Geschichte des Berufsbildungsgesetzes 1875-1981, Cologne/Vienna 1983

31 Cf. Nolte, H./H.-J. Röhrs (Publisher): Das Berufsbildungsgesetz. Text und Diskussion 1969-1976, Bad Heilbronn 1979

much later, this date marked the end of an era in vocational training in Germany.

1.3 The development phase of the dual vocational training system (as from 1970): Government influence and rationalisation

In the opinion of numerous experts on vocational training we can only speak of a dual system of vocational training in the Federal Republic of Germany since the Vocational Training Act entered into force in 1969. This Act not only brought together the previously splintered training legislation, but also removed a whole number of legal uncertainties and allowed extensive rationalisation of the training system which had grown up. With this Act the state also secured itself a certain amount of influence on vocational training once again following some decades in which this had been considered essentially a ''matter for the private sector'', i.e. the entrepreneurs.

It was not so much the entry into force of the Vocational Training Act which marked the beginning of a new epoch in 1970, but rather a different problem to which a hectic attempt was made to react with a ''vocational education reform''. The problem was the removal of traditional structures which occurred in the early seventies due to the socio-economic modernisation process and which therefore no longer stabilised the traditional training and vocational choice behaviour of large population groups[32]. The resulting general thrust towards grammar schools and university in the seventies and eighties could not take place in Germany simply because the worsening of the employment situation as a result of the global economic crisis and the problem of providing education for the baby boom generations caused a massive slow-down in the expansion of training oriented towards extending access to universities, if it did not stop it altogether. Since the early 1990s the fall in the numbers in each year which has allowed students to move relatively freely in the existing training institutions is now allowing ''meritocratic'' logic (B. Lutz), i.e. the sole social and vocational allocation of positions via general schools and their leaving certificates, to take full effect, and is beginning to threaten the continued existence of the dual system, at least in the medium term.

---

32   Cf. Lutz, B.: Der kurze Traum immerwährender Prosperität, Frankfurt/New York 1984

The necessary reforms would have had to have been carried out in the 1970s, but the education policy restrictions of the social partners and the bureaucracy, its short-sighted attachment to separate interests allowed only a rationalisation of the dual system[33]. Today, twenty years later, the change is forging ahead of its own accord as a crisis-ridden process of adaptation.

The fragmented pre-1969 training legislation defined vocational training as chiefly being an issue for "the private sector", meaning that vocational training was largely subject to the restrictive interest policy of employers and the representatives of these interests in society, and did not appear as a "public task". The enormous reform efforts in the field of vocational training which commenced at the beginning of the seventies, however, are not directly due to the adoption of the VTA. On the contrary, the Act was more of an obstacle to the reformers and two attempts were made to introduce amendments[34]. In retrospect, however, it is clear that the Vocational Training Act – despite its conservative inclination – was able to provide a frame-work for outstanding modernisation of training in Western Germany.

This commences with the responsibility for (in-company) vocational training: the traditional rights of the Chambers of Trade regarding vocational training had to be handed over to government responsibility; since 1973 this area has been coordinated by the Federal Minister for Education and Science (BMBW)*, the corresponding sectoral ministries being only responsible for recognising the training trades (vocations). The BMBWT is responsible for coordinating the Vocational Training Act, for basic issues of vocational training policy; it is the senior authority for the Federal Vocational Training Institute and is directly responsible for decreeing regulations on further vocational training and the teaching qualifications of trainers.

The one-sided influence of employers on vocational training was replaced, by law, by a system of differentiated responsibility which, however, leaves much to be desired. The Federation, the individual states, the trade unions and, to a limited extent, also the vocational school teachers participate at

---

33 Cf. Lipsmeier, A. (Publisher): Berufsbildungspolitik in den 70er Jahren, Wiesbaden 1983
34 Cf. Faulstich, P.: Interessenkonflikte um die Berufsbildung, Weinheim/Basel 1977;
*) Since 1994: Ministry of Education, Science, Research and Technology (BMBWT)

different levels in planning, implementing and controlling vocational training[35].

Since 1977 the training market has also become decisively more transparent. The annual vocational training report informs on the regional and sectoral trends in providing training places and the demand for such places; it also estimates anticipated developments in available training places in the coming years. A vocational training statistic combined with the report gives information and chief data and trends on vocational training. A Federal Vocational Training Research Institute was set up through the VTA to carry out research and development tasks in the field of vocational training. The extended mandate of the successor institution, the Federal Vocational Training Institute, is defined in an amendment law to the VTA, the 1981 Vocational Training Support Act (Berufsbildungförderungsgesetz §§6-18). The new institutions and instruments opened the way for some of the chief problems of the dual vocational training to be tackled and the "system" became fixed and rationalised. Since 1972, for example, the federal training regulations for in-company training and the "Länder" framework curricula for school training have been coordinated in a special procedure[36]; a large-scale development programme for industry-wide training establishments has widely solved the problem of qualification deficits chiefly felt in the manual trades training, and the teaching qualification for in-company trainers has been formally regulated by decree since 1972.

Furthermore, decisive rationalisation work was carried out in the field of training vocations: since 1969 new training regulations have been enacted for 250 training vocations (from a total of 374 as per 1993). 97% of all trainees in these vocations are incorporated in this system. A second "modernisation" wave which will particularly cover the training vocations that were reorganised at the beginning of the mid-1970s will be the focal point of reorganisation work in the 1990s (Berufsbildungsbericht 1990). One development, which had been the goal of educational policy commitment as early as the beginning of the 1970s, became stabilised in the course of this regulatory work: in practically all training regulations standardised basic training and a differentiated specialised training were separated. The re-

---

35 Cf. Götz, H.: Berufsbildungsrecht, Munich 1992
36 Cf. Benner, H./F. Püttmann: 20 Jahre Gemeinsames Ergebnisprotokoll. Published by BMBW in co-operation with the KMK, (Bonn 1992)

formers of the seventies wanted to standardise basic vocational training, add to it some expedient general contents, and incorporate it in the vocational schools which, with a new full-time entrance stage, the basic vocational training year (the Berufsgrundbildungsjahr-BGJ), would have given a new modern structure to the dual system. The BGJ, however, only became partially accepted: the employer organisations and industry feared a "state control" of vocational training, and generated enormous political resistance[37].

The Basic Vocational Training Year was only an approach towards comprehensively reforming the vocational training system. The "College Grading Trial of North-Rhine Westphalia" and the concept of the Berlin Uppergrade Centres may also be mentioned. These innovations that arose in the course of the general expansion and reform of training were all more or less failures. However, their legitimation consisted of the fact that they all addressed the weakness of the dual system: their goal was to improve the quality of practical vocational training and finally to link vocational training to the general qualification system. A major aspect of the intended reform was that the vocational schools which were undergoing almost inflationary differentiation were to be related in a legitimated overall concept.

The dual system is in a remarkably ambiguous situation: on the one hand it is enjoying unsurpassed public and international esteem, due primarily to the high proportions of each generational year taken by the dual system but also to its closeness to practice and low costs. It is therefore hardly surprising that on 1 September 1990 this training system was extended unchanged to the former East Germany and East Berlin. On the other hand, signs of its decline cannot be ignored; these include:

• a decline in the number of applicants, in some cases dramatic,
• a fall in the average entry qualifications of applicants,
• a massive increase in the drop-out rate,
• increased numbers of trainees leaving the profession on qualification, and

---

37   Cf. Greinert, W.-D.: Das Berufsgrundbildungsjahr. Weiterentwicklung oder Ablösung des „dualen" Systems der Berufsausbildung?, Fankfurt/New York 1984

- the increasing abandonment of the dual system by industry, mainly for cost reasons due to global competitive pressures.

If it continues, this last trend could signal the beginning of the end of the dual system of vocational education and training in Germany[38].

---

38   Cf. Greinert, W.-D.: The "German System" of Vocational Education. History, Organization, Prospects, Baden-Baden 1994

Basic structure of the Educational system in the Federal Republic of Germany in 1990

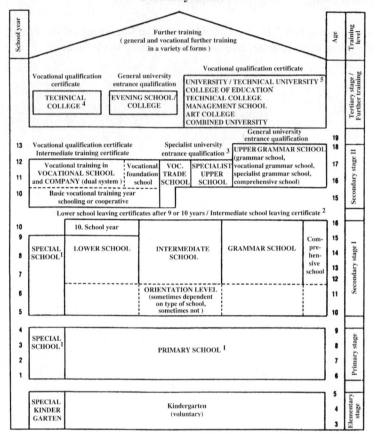

Diagrammatic representation. Systems depart in some countries. Movement between types of schools is always guaranteed if certain requirements are met. Compulsory full-time schooling is for 9 years (10 years in BE and NW), compulsory part-time schooling for 3 years.

1   Special schools with different sections according to the type of disability in the area of general and vocational schools.
2   Adults can obtain these certificates subsequently at evening classes.
3   College entrance qualifications can also be acquired at specialist vocational schools, vocational schools, etc.
4   Duration 1-3 years; including health service schools providing initial vocational training for careers in the health service and nursing.
5   Including universities with individual university courses (e.g. theology, philosophy, medicine, management science, sport).

2 The functional elements of the dual system: Training market and vocational training legislation

If we return to the ''place-of-learning'' criterion, it is indeed appropriate to question the term ''dual system'' in defining vocational training in the Federal Republic of Germany, because from this viewpoint it is assumed that ''two places of learning of equal value and of the same standard are combined together to form a ''system'' – an integrated whole with clear functionalisation of the individual ''parts''[39]. According to our differentiation criterion, however, the ''parts'' are not the two places of learning but the training market and the vocational training legislation, which indeed combine to form an ''integrated whole with clear functionalisation''. We, therefore, call these the functional elements of the dual system which first have to be described and analyzed.

2.1 The training market in the Federal Republic of Germany

The training market in the Federal Republic of Germany has the character of a supply market in which the following suppliers offer training places: industry and trade, manual trades, agriculture, civil service, freelance professions, domestic science and ocean navigation. The suppliers (= companies) offer their training places on a voluntary basis; companies are under no obligation to provide training services.

According to the most recent workplace survey[40] some 513,000 companies (of a total of 2.6 million) provided training. Small companies and practices with a maximum of 4 employees naturally provide less training. Companies employing 5-9 persons, however, account for 40 %. In the category 10 – 199 employees the percentage of companies carrying out training rises to 50 % to 75 %. Nevertheless, 13 % of companies employing more than 1,000 persons do not provide training[41].

---

39   Cf. Stratmann, K.: Das duale System und das Problem seiner ''Verschulung'', in: Die Deutsche Berufs- und Fachschule 71 (1975), 820-835, p. 823
40   Workplace census of 25 May 1987
41   Cf. Werner, R.: 10 % der Auszubildenden in Großbetrieben, in: Berufsbildung in Wissenschaft und Praxis 19 (1990), No 4, p. 35

In 1987, 10 % of trainees received their qualifications in the latter companies – with more than 1,000 employees. Approximately half of the trainees (52 %) had a contract with a company employing up to 50 employees. One third of all trainees received their training in companies with 5-20 employees, a size category in which small manual trade enterprises are chiefly represented. This size category can be defined as the main group of training enterprises, this also being indicated by the training rate (ratio of trainees to employees), which was approximately 10 %. **Table 1** indicates the percentage of trainees in the different company size categories and the total training rate[42].

Table 1: Trainees according to company size category

Workplaces with ... to ... people[1]	Trainees as % of training rate[2]		
	1970	1987	1987
1 – 4	10.3	7.1	6.0
5 – 9	19.2	18.6	10.2
10 – 19	14.0	15.7	9.8
20 – 49	13.8	14.1	7.2
50 – 99	8.8	8.7	5.8
100 – 199	8.2	8.2	5.6
200 – 499	9.7	10.9	5.8
500 – 999	16.0	6.8	5.9
1000+		9.8	4.8
Total	100.0	100.0	6.5

1 including trainees,
2 ratio of trainees to employees in percent, the category 1-4 employees does not include 'mini' enterprises with up to 2 employees (including trainees).

Source: Berufsbildung in Wissenschaft und Praxis (Vocational training in Science and Practice) 19 (1990), 4, p. 35.

According to an earlier survey[43] "large" suppliers of training places include:

• Steel-working, mechanical engineering and automotive engineering factories

---

42 Ditto, p. 35
43 Cf. Hofbauer, H./F. Stooß: Defizite und Überschüsse an betrieblichen Ausbildungsplätzen nach Wirtschafts- und Berufsgruppen, in: Mitteilungen aus der Arbeitsmarkt- und Berufsforschung 8 (1975), 101-135

- Trade and auxiliary industries, publishing and press
- Building trade
- Electrical engineering, precision mechanics and optics
- Woodworking, paper and printing industry
- Food, drink and tobacco industry
- Iron and non-ferrous metal industry, foundries
- Banking and insurance
- Other service industries
- Chemical industry, oil, plastics, rubber and asbestos processing
- Territorial authorities and insurances
- Hotel and restaurant*

* (Priority rated according to the number of occupied training places for male trainees.)

The offer for initial vocational training in the scope of the dual system that training companies can place on the training market is comprehensively regulated by legislation. According to §§ 25 and 28 of the VTA, training may only be given in state-recognised training vocations in accordance with authorized training plans. 374 training vocations were registered in the "Register of state-recognised training vocations" in 1993, 250 of which were recognised on the basis of the VTA[44]. At that time, 3 % of trainees were trained in accordance with training regulations which had been in existence prior to the VTA. It was the intention of the bodies that the regulatory reforms be considerably accelerated in future.

This legislative standardisation of training offered does not exclude variations

1. in regard to structure and the region;
2. in regard to quality per vocational field and company involved and
3. in regard to quantity depending on the economic situation.

The chance of obtaining a training place varies greatly in the different labour exchange areas of the Federal Republic of Germany. Many districts have structural weaknesses, particularly the Saarland, Rhineland Palatinate, part of Lower Saxony, Schleswig-Holstein and also other regions. Young people in these areas suffer from the fact that only a small number

---

44   Cf. Berufsbildungsbericht 1994, Bonn 1994, p. 78

of places are available, not covering many varied vocations. In industrial, urban areas, however, a large number of training places are available in many different vocations. A considerable number of training places offered often remain vacant because of lacking demand[45].

From the quality aspect companies offering training places can be classified into two categories:

- in the first category training is given on the production line with low cost inputs, apprentices are used rather as ("cheap") manpower; nevertheless, some of the companies in this category do offer interesting employment opportunities.
- in the second category, off production training is provided (e. g. in teaching workshops); this training is of a relatively high quality, but also entails high cost inputs.

It is difficult exactly to delimit these two categories because the features of the first category apply equally to a large section of the manual trades, commerce, agriculture, domestic science, freelance professions and also for individual branches and enterprises in industry[46]. It can be roughly estimated that the first category incorporates 85-90 % of all training places, the rest being in the second category. Numerous empirical surveys have indicated that the size of the company is a major factor influencing the quality of training places. Taking into account specific quality criteria, a certain critical company-size seems to be decisive from the vocational training aspect – companies with 25-99 employees, and a vocational training turning point is reached when the company has more than 100 employees, all criteria for a high quality training existing above this mark[47].

The users (= the trainees), of course, prefer those companies with the attractive training places and/or workplaces, which means that only these companies can promulgate their own active offer policy on the market for training places. They can exploit the demand potential according to their needs,

45   Cf. Schwarz, U./F. Stooß: Zur regionalen Ungleichheit der regionalen Bildungschancen und Vorschläge zum Abbau des Gefälles, in: Mitteilungen zur Arbeitsmarkt- und Berufsforschung 6 (1973), 121-176; jährliches regionales Angebot in: Berufsbildungsbericht
46   Cf. Steinbach S.: Analyse der Konjunkturabhängigkeit der betrieblichen Berufsausbildung in der Bundesrepublik Deutschland, Bonn 1974, p. 76 ff.
47   Stratmann, loc. cit., p. 833

and vary the quantity of places offered, and have a more pro-cyclic reaction to fluctuations in the economic cycle. The less attractive companies, particularly in the craft trades, commerce and service sectors act as a training reserve – assuming a normal demand situation[48]. As their main reason for training apprentices is to save on labour costs, they absorb the remainder of the demand potential in a very flexible way – independently of any fluctuations in the economic cycle (i.e. they have a "sponge function"). They are not usually able to promulgate an active offer policy.

The users in the training place market are juveniles with very different educational backgrounds[49]:

– without a lower school leaving certificate (2.8 %)
– possessing a lower school leaving certificate (36.6 %)
– holding the intermediate school leaving certificate or equivalent (31.8 %)
– holding university or college entrance qualification (14.5 %)
– holding a certificate of the basic vocational school year (Berufsgrundbildungsjahr) (4.2 %)
– holding a certificate from a vocational training centre (Berufssfachschule) (9.3 %)
– holding a certificate from the preparatory vocational year (0.9 %)

In the former East Germany most trainees (65.8 %) still come from the 10-year Polytechnic Upper Schools or comparable schools, which give out intermediate school leaving certificates. At 4.2 % the equivalent of "A" level students (Abiturienten) make up only a small proportion of trainees in the dual system. In the former West Germany the proportion of trainees made up of "A" level equivalent students exhibited a constant increase up to 1991 (14.6 %); but since 1992 a greater inclination to study (including amongst female students) can be seen.

The proportion of lower school leavers reaches its highest level (60 %) in manual trades trainees; in trade and industry the biggest group is made up

---

48 This was not the case in the Federal Republic of Germany from c. 1974-1986; the demographically rooted excess demand led to extensive increases in the training quotas, particularly for manual trades. (1980: 40.9 %), dropping since then (1988: 34.9 %)
49 Berufsbildungsbericht 1994, p. 60

of intermediate school leavers (33.7 %). In the civil service and the free-lance professions over 50 % of trainees come from intermediate and comparable schools[50].

The average age of the trainees rose during the period 1970 to 1988 from 16.6 to 18.7 years of age. Whereas in 1970 only approximately every fifth trainee (22 %) was 18 years or older, these now make up two-thirds (68 %) of trainees. There is only a small difference in age between female and male trainees. The average age of apprentices, which has increased quite steadily since the mid seventies, is chiefly all due to the changed educational behaviour. It is characterised by a demand for higher general school qualifications and a greater interest in a dual vocational training by school leavers holding high-level formal school leaving certificates[51].

An annual survey of school leavers provides information on the change in the training behaviour of school leavers. The results indicate the intended transfers from schooling to training at the end of the school year, and generally pinpoint strong preferences for training within the dual system. Approx. 47 % of one age-group transferred to the dual system in 1976, approx. 60 % in 1989, and in 1989 the dual system received 70 %. The easing of the situation in the training place-market has lead to an increase in the percentage of persons wanting to change directly from the general school into the dual system, the ''deviation'' via attending a full-time vocational training centre, being chosen ever less frequently[52].

Supply and demand in the dual vocational training sector are largely harmonized by the labour exchanges, who hold the monopoly on vocational consultancy and labour placement in the Federal Republic of Germany. Details of the vacancies registered by the companies and the number of applicants that are centrally registered by the Federal Labour Office are annually documented in the Vocational Consultancy Statistics as part of the Vocational Training Report and provide an overview of supply and demand within the dual system as at September 30 of each year[53].

---

50 Ditto, p. 60 f.
51 Berufsbildungsbericht 1990, p. 42, 48 f.
52 Cf. Berufsbildungsbericht 1986, p. 32 ff.
53 Cf. Table 15

According to the latest Vocational Training Report (1994), the demand for training places in Germany in 1993 amounted to some 588,000, of which 486,000 emanated from the ''old'' Federal States and 102,000 from the ''new'' Federal States. The supply of training places in the ''old'' Federal states has fallen since 1984 (726,786), not consistently but overall, but in 1993 still amounted to 554,626 training places. This equates to 114.2 training places for every 100 applicants. In the ''new'' Federal states the supply of training places has increased by just over 3 % on the previous year, but this still does not meet demand.

The number of training courses implemented from 1960 to 1992 is shown in **Table 2**. The first column clearly indicates excess demand during the decade from 1976 to 1986, due to the high demographic figures, when the number of training contracts entered into also greatly increased; this is widely used as evidence for the performance capability and flexibility of the dual system. The trade unions calculate, however, that between 1980 and 1984 alone, 563,000 young people did not receive full and complete vocational training, and that this was chiefly due to the lacking absorption capacity of the dual system[54].

The above average increase in training contracts in craft trades and in agriculture is also evident – this being critically interpreted as ,mismanagement'', i.e. the training of surplus labour in trades where the market did not require labour in the short term, or which were not forward looking[55]. This trend is, however, counteracted by an opposing tendency when the high-birth-rate years entered vocational training; the training structures clearly shifted – partly towards global trends on the employment sector[56].

Nevertheless, the term ''mismanagement'' or ''misstructuring'' marks a negative characteristic of the dual training system of the Federal Republic of Germany. In view of the fact that the vocational training is financed at single-company level, cost considerations are of primary importance for decision-making by the companies[57]; consequently, global qualification requirements of the employment system are largely ignored, or avoided.

---

54 Cf. Berufsbildungsbericht 1986, p. 21
55 Frackmann, M.: Fachkräftebedarf und Berufsausbildung, Cologne/Vienna 1982, p. 135
56 Berufsbildungsbericht 1988, p. 45 ff.
57 Cf. Final report ''Kosten und Finanzierung der außerschulischen beruflichen Bildung'', Bonn 1974, p. 356 f.

Table 2: Trainees according to training categories in thousands

Year	Trainees (total)							
	Total	Of which in training area						
		trade & industry	manual trades	agriculture	civil service[1,2]	freelance professions[2]	domestic science[2]	ocean navigation[2]
	Former West Germany							
1960	[illeg.]	743.1	446.6	36.3	19.4	20.4	6.0	7.0
1965	[illeg.]	752.4	468.0	37.3	23.7	45.5	6.5	5.0
1970	1268.7	724.9	419.5	38.1	20.2	56.4	7.2	2.4
1975	1328.9	634.0	504.7	33.0	46.0	103.2	7.3	0.9
1980	1715.5	786.9	702.3	46.8	53.8	114.3	7.6	1.0
1981	1676.9	771.3	673.6	46.5	54.3	123.6	6.6	0.9
1982	1675.9	764.7	665.5	49.6	58.3	128.5	8.4	0.8
1983	1722.4	791.9	674.9	52.0	63.7	129.7	8.8	0.9
1984	1800.1	841.1	693.2	53.2	69.2	132.4	9.9	1.0
1985	1831.3	874.6	687.5	53.4	72.6	131.5	10.6	1.1
1986	1805.2	882.2	657.8	50.2	73.1	129.9	11.0	1.1
1987	1738.7	866.0	617.8	44.6	71.7	125.1	12.8	0.8
1988	1658.0	827.2	577.9	38.5	67.3	133.6	12.9	0.6
1989	1552.5	783.3	532.5	33.8	62.2	129.3	11.0	0.5
1990	1476.9	756.4	486.9	29.7	63.4	130.3	9.7	0.4
1991	1430.2	734.3	460.4	27.4[3]	61.8[3]	137.4[3]	8.3[3]	0.5
1992	1388.3	690.6	459.6	24.7[3]	62.0[3]	143.2[3]	7.9[3]	0.5
	"New" Federal States							
1990	255.5	*	*	*	*	*	*	*
1991	235.3	145.0	67.0	10.1[4]	3.6[4]	6.4[4]	2.8[4]	0.4
1992	278.3	151.0	93.9	8.3[4]	9.3[4]	11.4[4]	4.2[4]	0.2
	Germany (total)							
1990	1732.4	*	*	*	*	*	*	*
1991	1665.5	879.4	527.4	37.5	65.4	143.8	11.1	0.9
1992	1666.6	841.6	553.4	33.0	71.4	154.6	12.1	0.6

1 Excluding trainees whose training vocations are recorded under other responsible places under the Vocational Training Act

2 For the years 1960, 1965 and 1970 the information available is incomplete.

Considerable discrepancies thus arise between the training and the employment sectors.

According to an older survey[58], in 1970 the trades in which 75 % of the skilled workers were trained, only employed 40 % of these skilled workers;

Also: Trainees according to training categories in thousands

Year	Trainees (female) Total	Of which in training area						
		trade & industry	manual trades	agricul- ture	civil service [1,2]	free- lance profes- sions[2]	domes- tic science[2]	ocean naviga- tion[2]
	Former West Germany							
1960	460.7	327.9	96.6	12.0	1.3	17.0	6.0	–
1965	493.2	330.2	101.7	11.4	1.5	41.9	6.5	–
1970	449.1	293.8	81.7	9.2	1.7	55.3	7.2	0.04
1975	469.9	249.6	96.3	6.3	13.6	96.9	7.3	–
1980	655.0	343.7	157.2	11.8	22.8	109.2	7.5	0.01
1981	647.8	334.8	151.4	12.6	23.9	118.5	6.6	0.01
1982	654.0	326.2	154.2	15.1	27.1	123.2	8.3	0.01
1983	676.3	336.3	160.6	16.3	30.3	124.0	8.7	0.01
1984	718.9	361.8	171.0	16.5	33.0	126.6	9.9	0.02
1985	743.8	380.4	175.8	16.8	34.5	125.8	10.6	0.00
1986	746.2	384.5	175.7	16.0	34.9	124.2	10.9	0.02
1987	732.0	379.1	171.7	14.4	34.4	119.7	12.6	0.02
1988	713.8	363.6	163.6	12.9	32.5	128.7	12.6	0.02
1989	669.1	343.5	149.1	11.3	30.2	124.3	10.7	0.00
1990	629.8	324.6	131.5	9.8	29.6	124.9	9.5	0.00
1991	603.6	308.0	117.5	8.8[3]	29.9[3]	131.3[3]	8.1[3]	0.01
1992	577.4	287.5	107.0	7.8[3]	31.2[3]	136.2[3]	7.7[3]	0.01
	"New" Federal states							
1990	97.4	*	*	*	*	*	*	–
1991	89.2	62.4	11.6	4.8[4]	1.6[4]	6.2[4]	2.6[4]	–
1992	103.3	64.1	15.2	4.5[4]	4.9[4]	10.5[4]	4.0[4]	–
	Germany (total)							
1990	727.2	*	*	*	*	*	*	0.00
1991	692.8	370.4	129.1	13.6	31.5	137.4	10.8	0.01
1992	680.8	351.6	122.2	12.3	36.2	146.8	11.7	0.01

3 Including East Berlin.   4 Excluding East Berlin.

Source: Grund- und Strukturdaten 1994/95, page 100 f.

vice versa, at the same time, approximately 51 % of the skilled workers were employed in jobs for which next generation workers were only trained to a small extent, or not at all.

---

58   Cf. Hofbauer/Stooß, loc. cit. (Anmerkung 43)

2.2 Vocational Training Legislation in the Federal Republic of Germany

As already mentioned a special vocational training legislation, the second functional element of the dual system, has only existed in the Federal Republic since 1st September 1969. Before this date, the legal regulations on vocational training were chiefly integrated into economic laws[59], a tradition from which the federal legislator also derives its responsibility also for VTA[60]. The following legislation, which also affects vocational training in part, are also Federal legislative directives – pursuant to article 74, No. 11 and 12 of the Basic Law:

- The Labour Support Act (Arbeitsförderungsgesetz – AFG) of 25 June 1969
- The Industrial Relations Act (Betriebsverfassungsgesetz) of 15 January, 1972
- The Trades Regulation Act (Handwerksordnung) in the version of 28.12.1965, most recently amended by Article 43 of the Act, dated 28.6.1990.
- Youth Labour Protection Act (Gesetz zum Schutze der arbeitenden Jugend – JArbSchG), of 9.89.1960 in the version of 12.04.1976
- The Act governing the temporary regulation of the Law on Chambers of Industry and Commerce (Gesetz zur vorläufigen Regelung des Rechts der Industrie- und Handelskammern) dated 18.12.1956 in the version as amended by the Vocational Training Act
- The Vocational Training Support Act (Berufsbildungsförderungsgesetz – BerBiFG) dated 23.12.1981, in the version amended by the "First Law to Modify the BerBiFG" dated 4.12.1986.

In the new Federal states the following is also to be noted:

- Treaty by the Federal Republic of Germany and the German Democratic Republic creating the Unification of Germany (Unification Treaty) of 31.08.90

---

59 Cf. Wentzel, M.: Autonomes Berufsausbildungsrecht und Grundgesetz, Stuttgart 1970; Richter, I.: Öffentliche Verantwortung für die berufliche Bildung, Stuttgart 1970

60 The Federation derives its competence for vocational training from Article 74, Nos. 11 and. Nr. 12 Constitution – Grundgesetz (GG)

The central legal basis for vocational training in the dual system is the Vocational Training Act – VTA (Berufsbildungsgesetz – BBiG) of 14.8.1969. The second part of the Trade Regulations, which deals with vocational training, was modified with the adoption of the Vocational Training Act anal substantively adapted to the provisions of the Act (cf. VTA, Section 100), so that a uniform legal basic applied to all training areas.

The VTA is a relatively comprehensive Act containing 113 Sections divided into 9 parts

Part 1: General regulations
Part 2: Vocational training relationship
Part 3: Order of the vocational training
Part 4: Vocational training committees
Part 5: Vocational Training Research (cancelled, newly regulated by the Vocational Training Support Act)
Part 6: Special regulations for individual branches of the economy and trades
Part 7: Regulations concerning fines
Part 8: Modifications and invalidity of regulations
Part 9: Temporary and final regulations.

Parts 2 and 3 form the legal core of the Act, because, as explained in the introductory chapter, these two parts reflect the actual duality of the system in their specific structure geared to vocational training legislation: Part 2, the private law sphere of the market, Part 3 the public-law sphere of the State. Consequently the Labour Courts are responsible for legal conflicts concerning Section 2 – Vocational Training Contract, whereas the Administrative Courts are responsible for legal conflicts concerning Section 3 – Order. Part 1 of the Act essentially regulates its area of purview, Part 4 lays down some co-determination rights of social groups in vocational training.

The Act regulates "Vocational Training" in so far as it is not implemented in vocational training schools, which are subject to the school laws of the individual states (Länder) (Section 2, Sub-section 1). It does not apply to vocational training for public employees or vocational training on merchant ships (Section 2, sub-section 2). Under the terms of the Vocational Training Act, vocational education comprises vocational training (initial training), vocational further education and job retraining (VTA section 1, sub-section 1).

47

From the legal viewpoint, the young people learning in the dual system are on the one hand students – in the public Berufsschule (vocational school) – and on the other hand, pursuant to BBiFG, they are employees with the special legal status of trainees. This special legal status is based on a training contract, which must, by law, be entered into when a vocational training relationship is established (Section 3, sub-section 1). The essential points of the contract are to be laid down in writing (Section 4, sub-section 1); the document must include at least the following details:

1. The type of training and its organization as far as time and subject matter are concerned, as well as the objectives of training and in particular the type of job for which the apprentice is to be trained.
2. The starting date and length of training
3. The training to be done outside the place of training,
4. The length of regular daily training
5. The length of the probationary period
6. The payment and amount of wages
7. The length of vacation period
8. The conditions under which the vocational training contract can be terminated (Section 4,1)

The type of vocational training and the objectives are geared to the skills and knowledge listed in the vocational profile, the organization of the vocational training in regard to time and subject matter, is laid down in the Training Guidelines (Ausbildungsrahmenplan – Section 25,2), whose contents are to be geared to the particular characteristics of the firm. A vocational training relationship should not exceed 3 years and not be shorter than 2 years. The duration depends, however, on the specific set of training regulations for the individual trades, and is usually longer nowadays in the new vocations (3.5 years).

The training relationship begins with a probationary period which must last at least one month and not more than three months (Section 13). During the probationary period, the vocational training relationship can be terminated at any time without notice (Section 15,2). The trainee has a right to payment during his/her training, the rates being governed by Sections 10, 11 and 12 of the Vocational Training Act, although these are only guidelines. The two parties to the contract are free to set the amount of payment, and generally concur with current union agreements. The vacation entitlement for trainees is also generally determined under trade union-management agreements; the general governing guidelines are the pertinent provisions of the Youth Labour Protection Act (Jugendarbeitsschutzgesetz) and the Federal Vacation Act (Bundesurlaubsgesetz).

In addition to regulations concerning the duties and obligations of the contracting parties (Sections 6 and 9) and special termination regulations (Section 15), a number of other protective clauses are laid down by law in favour of the trainee, such as, for example, the prohibition of demanding an "apprenticeship premium", the agreement on contractual penalties or the exclusion of claims for remuneration of damage (Section 5). The training company is also obliged to give the trainee leave to participate in training at the Vocational School and to attend examinations (Section 7), and to issue him/her with a reference upon termination of the vocational training relationship (Section 8).

The Order system for vocational training law as laid down in the VTA is chiefly supported by two components: firstly the regulatory powers of the Chambers (‚Competent bodies", Section 44), and secondly the institution of the state-recognized training trades (Section 25). Pursuant to Sections 75 and 64 and 87, 89 and 91 of the VTA, the pertinent Chambers are the "responsible authorities" for vocational training in the so-called "large training areas"; industry/trade and crafts and also in agriculture and the free professions, and these Chambers (‚the Chambers of Commerce and Industry" and "Chambers of Trade", "Chambers of Agriculture", etc.), therefore, possess the regulatory powers. Various Federal and State authorities function as the responsible authority only in the domestic science and public service sectors (Sections 84 and 93).

Chambers are commercial associations that are financed by their members – the companies. However, they are also corporations under public law, and subject to the legal supervision of the Supreme State (Land) Authority. The chambers do not have a specialized supervisory body. According to Section 44 of the VTA, the responsible authority regulates the entire implementation of vocational training in the companies pursuant to the legislation should other regulations not exist. – This involves the following tasks:

– supervising of the implementation of vocational training pursuant to Section 45, including the appointment of training counsellors

- the promotion of vocational training through counselling for the training firms and the trainees pursuant to Section 45
- aptitude testing of the training company pursuant to Section 23
- aptitude testing of the trainers pursuant to Section 23
- approval of reduction or prolongation of training periods (Section 29)
- the establishment and upkeep of the register of vocational training contracts (Sections 31-33)
- the establishment of examination committees and holding of final and intermediate examinations (Sections 36 and 41)
- the admission of trainees to the final examination (Section 39, 40)
- the issuing of examination regulations (Section 41)
- the establishment of an arbitration authority to settle conflicts between trainers and trainees arising from an existing training relationship (Section 102 VTA in connection with Section 111,2 of the Labour Court Law)

The focal areas of this catalogue of tests concern (1.) the Chambers' contacts with the companies, and their tasks of supervising, Provide counselling and aptitude testing and (2.) the holding of examinations. The legislative directives on which these activities are based vary in detail: whereas the supervision, counselling and aptitude testing of companies and trainers is regulated in a very open and formal manner and the Chambers enjoy a wide scope of action in interpreting the actual training situation, the area of "examinations" is regulated in great detail, particularly in regard to the composition of the examination boards, their appointment and activities (Sections 37 and 38). These regulations stipulate that the same employee and employer sides must provide an equal number of members to represent them on the examination boards, plus at least one teacher from a vocational school (Section 37,2). The examination regulations of the Chambers have to be approved by the competent Supreme state authority (Section 41).

In accordance with the principle of exclusivity in Section 28 VTA, young people under 18 years of age can only be trained in recognized training trades, and the training itself must conform with the valid training regulations. Training trades can receive official recognition by legal regulation of the competent sectoral minister (e. g. the Economic Affairs Minister for Vocational Trades) in agreement with the Federal Minister for Education, Science, Research and Technology – pursuant to Section 25 of the VTA;

the sectoral minister can also cancel recognition. The sectoral minister also decrees the pertinent training regulations[61].

The training regulations should contain the following details at least (Section 25,2):

- the name of the training trade
- the duration of training
- the skills and knowledge that are the object of the vocational training (vocational profile)
- an instruction concerning the time-input for and organization of the skills and knowledge (general training guideline)
- the examination requirements

The initiatives for developing a vocational training trade or for revising training plans mostly derive from the associations and national organizations of the companies and the trade unions. While, in principle, anyone can make recommendations concerning training plans, in practice, recommendations are not submitted to the specialized ministries without involving the trade associations and the national organizations[62].

The complicated procedure for drawing up training regulations and coordinating them with the general regulations (of the vocational schools) provides proof of the central importance the vocational trade has as an institution in the educational legislation in Germany.

- a preliminary procedure
- a working and coordination procedure
- a decree procedure.

The preliminary procedure commences with the so-called "application talks" on the regulation with the specialised minister. Participants: the Federal Minister for Education, Science, Research and Technology (BM-BWT), the national and specialized organisations of the employers and em-

---

61 Cf. Benner, H.: Der Ausbildungsberuf als berufspädagogisches und bildungsökonomisches Problem, Hanover 1977
62 Bundesministerium für Bildung und Wissenschaft (Publisher): Ausbildungsordnungen. Erläuterungen und Hinweise zur Erarbeitung von Ausbildungsordnungen nach dem Berufsbildungsgesetz und der Handwerksordnung, (Bonn 1986), p. 7

ployees, the Federal Institute for Vocational Training and the Permanent Conference of State Ministers of Cultural Affairs (KMK). The aim of the talks is to lay down the ''basic values'' for the project[63]. On the basis of these basic values, the Federal Institute for Vocational Training drafts a project application for national-state coordination. The specialized minister drafts the project application in agreement with the BMBWT. The BM-BWT, in agreement with the specialized ministry, applies for the project in the Coordination Committee for ''Training Regulations / Training Guidelines'' set up pursuant to the Joint Protocol of 30.05.1972, this committee incorporating representatives of the Federation and the States.

Once the Coordination Committee has resolved on the project, the elaboration and coordination Procedure commences, which will not be described in this context[64]. The project is finalized by the decree procedure, in which the responsible Federal Minister, in agreement with the BMBWT – and following examination of legal aspects the Federal Minister of Justice – decrees the training regulation, and publishes it in the Federal Journal. The training guidelines for vocational schools is adopted by the KMK and passed on to the Ministers/Senators responsible for Cultural Affairs.

Up to now, three training regulation concepts have crystallised

• Concept 1:
training vocations without specialisation (mono-vocations)

• Concept 2:
training regulations with specialisation, in the form of areas of specialization or areas of key emphasis

• Concept 3:
Several training vocations with training certification in the scope of a cumulative training

---

63 Ditto, p. 9: Basic values are in particular: the name of the trade, the duration of training, the allocation to vocational field, the data on structure and development of the training course, the description of the trade, the time-table, other procedures.
64 Ditto, p. 10 f; Benner H.: Ordnung der staatlich anerkannten Ausbildungsberufe, Berlin 1982, p. 65 ff.

Concept 2 was primarily used in the reform procedure completed for the large training areas of metalworking and electrical engineering in industry and trade[65], although several training vocations or even an entire vocational area were compiled in one regulation. Cumulative training (cf. Section 26 of the VTA) is available in the building trade[66] and in the textile industry. This cumulative training was again abandoned in the electrical engineering trades, which, in our opinion, means that this progressive method of training, which was expressly anchored in 1969 in the VTA, no longer possesses any orientation value.

Part 4 of the VTA regulates the right of participation in designing vocational training, particularly that of social groupings other than the employers. Under this regulation, so-called "Vocational Training Committees" are to be set up at the responsible authority, consisting of six employer representatives, six employee representatives and six teachers at vocational training schools, the teachers having consultative votes (cf. Section 56,1). The Vocational Training Committees have to be informed and consulted on all important matters concerning vocational training (Section 58,1) and resolve on the legal regulations governing the implementation of vocational training, to be decreed by the responsible authority (Section 58,2), e. g. the examination regulations.

While these committees of the Chambers have consultative and voting rights, the "State Vocational Training Committees" set up at the State Governments have purely consultative capacities (Section 54). They consist of an equal number of representatives of the employers, the employees, and the supreme State authority; all members have to possess expertise in issues concerning vocational training.

---

65 Cf. e.g. Regulation on the vocational training in industrial electrical engineering trades and for communication electronics of the German Federal Post Office, dated January 15, 1987 (Federal Law Gazette I, p.199); Verordnung über die Berufsausbildung in den industriellen Metallberufen, vom 15. Januar 1987 (Federal Law Gazette I, p. 274)
66 Cf. e.g. Bode, R.: Berufliche Erstausbildung in der Bauwirtschaft, Alsbach 1980

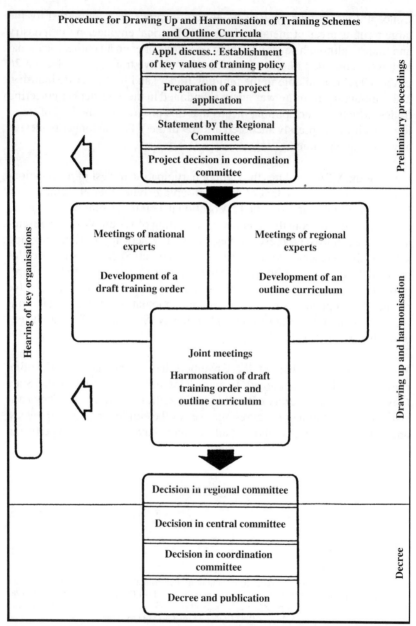

Procedure for Drawing Up and Harmonisation of Training Schemes and Outline Curricula

Appl. discuss.: Establishment of key values of training policy

Preparation of a project application

Statement by the Regional Committee

Project decision in coordination committee

Preliminary proceedings

Hearing of key organisations

Meetings of national experts

Development of a draft training order

Meetings of regional experts

Development of an outline curriculum

Joint meetings

Harmonsation of draft training order and outline curriculum

Drawing up and harmonisation

Decision in regional committee

Decision in central committee

Decision in coordination committee

Decree and publication

Decree

Source: Benner, Ordnung der staatlich anerkannten Ausbildungsberufe, p.67

54

The State Committees have to provide advice to the State governments on issues concerning vocational training, in particular, they have to induce cooperation between in-school and in-company vocational training, and to incorporate the needs of vocational training in any reform and on further development of the schooling system (Section 55).

Following the dissolution of the Federal Vocational Training Committees the advisory functions on vocational training to the Federal Government is taken on by the Main Committee of the Federal Vocational Training Institute (Section 8 of the Vocational Training Support Act), consisting of member representatives of the employers, the employees, the Federal States and the Federation (Section 8,2 BerBiFG).

The new order of industrial metal trades (vocational field principle, basic training principle, stages in training)

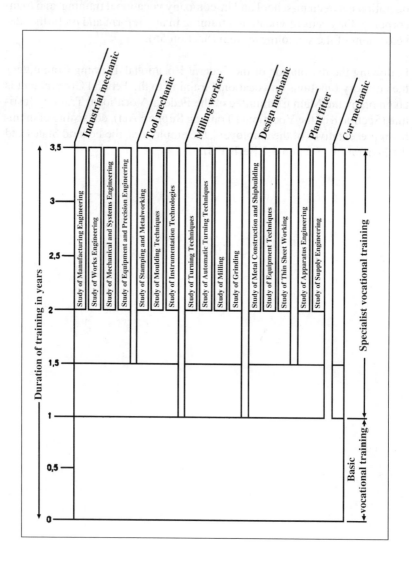

3 The places of learning in the dual system

Even though this chapter describes and analyses the structures of places of learning in the dual system, this does not mean in the final analysis that we quasi-silently accept the place of learning as a differentiation criterion for training systems. It is evident, however, that vocational training systems cannot be characterised without describing the institutional side, and this is just represented by the so-called "places of learning". It rapidly becomes apparent that the traditional rationale for the duality of the training system in the Federal Republic of Germany has become out-dated anyway, because, the industry-wide training workshops at least have become established as a new place of learning with an independent character, which the term "dual" obviously ignores.

Neither can the traditional division of labour between the company and the vocational school – imparting practical vocational knowledge on the one hand and theoretical vocational knowledge on the other – claim, in the meantime, to provide information on the institutional peculiarity or diversity of the "dual" system.

3.1 The company as a place of learning

In the Federal Republic of Germany's dual training system, the company is by far the most important place of learning, if only viewed from the fact that approximately three-quarters of the training time is spent here[67]. Having already presented some general orientation data on the structure of training companies in Chapter 2, this chapter concentrates on the actual potential for vocation related learning in the companies of the different branches of training and the economy. The previous chapter already identified two areas or levels in regard to the quality of in-company training: one area where training is production-oriented and of low cost intensity, and another in which training takes place off production, systematically, with relatively high cost inputs. As it is difficult to delimit these areas exactly and impossible to weight them from the quantitative aspect, the following section attempts to typify in-company training, based on pertinent empirical investigations[68], although abstracted from reality.

---

67   Still some four-fifths fifteen years ago.

The highest quality form of vocational training in the dual system takes the form of industrial training in teaching workshops. Its chief characteristics are[69]:

- an independent training department exists staffed with full-time manager and full-time instructors; these persons are generally highly qualified;
- training takes place off production, in training workshops or other training rooms with sophisticated learning aids;
- systematic practical vocational training is given in the form of courses, networked courses or projects (= initial training); the specialised training is organised in the production departments according to a transfer plan;
- additional theory instruction is given to complement teaching in vocational schools; it is common for the training department to promote social, cultural and sports activities;
- trainees are recruited on the basis of specific aptitude tests;
- additional welfare assistance is provided by social workers, industrial psychologists etc.;
- the youth representatives on the workers council are given comprehensive participation rights with regard to training.

Training of the above type is provided particularly in large-scale industries (company size categories: 100-1000 and above 1000 employees), and here again particularly in the metalworking and electrical engineering industries and in the textile and chemical industries[70]. Table 3 indicates the exact distribution of company training workshops according to branch:

---

68 Cf. summarising older investigations: Lempert, W.: Neuere Untersuchungen zur Qualität der betrieblichen Lehre in der Bundesrepublik, in: Die Deutsche Berufs- und Fachschule 70 (1974), 68-84; more recent empirical investigations: Ziefuß, H.: Jugendliche in der gewerblich-technischen Ausbildung in Industrie und Handwerk, Kiel 1987; Damm-Rüger, S./U. Degen et al: Zur Struktur der betrieblichen Ausbildungsgestaltung (= Berichte zur beruflichen Bildung, No 101), Berlin/Bonn 1988; Berufsbildungsbericht 1990, p. 105 ff.
69 On the typisation of forms of training, cf. Mayer, E./W. Schumm et al: Betriebliche Ausbildung und gesellschaftliches Bewußtsein, Frankfurt/New York 1981, p. 54 ff.
70 Cf. Pätzold, G.: Auslese und Qualifikation. Institutionalisierte Berufsausbildung in westdeutschen Großbetrieben, Hanover 1977; Sonntag, K.: Inhalte und Strukturen industrieller Berufsausbildung, Frankfurt a. M. 1982

Table 3: Company training workshops (industry) according to branch

1. Construction, stone working, glass, ceramics	19
2. Metal	1,151
3. Electrical	277
4. Chemicals, plastics	81
5. Timber	5
6. Printing, paper	19
7. Textiles, clothing, leather	96
8. Food, drink and tobacco	2
9. Transport and supply	69
10. Other	1
All specialist areas	1,720

Source: Kleinschmidt, R.; In-company and industry-wide training workshops in the Federal Republic of Germany, Hanover 1974, page 30

In small and medium-sized industrial companies (company size categories: below 20, 20-100 employees) non-systematic industrial training is more usual. Its chief characteristics are:

- relatively low degree of automation and of organisation of the production process, consequently however, demands are relatively wide and versatile, i.e. average-to-good qualification potentials are offered; however, piecework may often be required, with low qualification potentials;
- production-orientation is the dominating organisational characteristic of the training; training is coordinated locally; the timing and content of training are structured along relatively general criteria;
- off-production training phases are usually possible; basic manual skills can be taught in so-called "training corners", which are organisationally attached to the operating department; part-time instructors
- theory teaching is left almost exclusively to the vocational school; the offer of in-company instruction depends greatly on the personal attitude of the production manager or instructor.

In all, the quality of training in small and medium-sized industrial companies depends largely on the interests and on the initiatives of individual persons or on the commitment of the workers' council and the trainees[71].

Traditional craftsmen training is most closely interlinked with the production process, it is often called "en-passant-" or "laissez-faire training". Its chief characteristics are:

- practical vocational qualification elements are taught almost exclusively on the job in the workshop or on the building site; "teaching corners" are seldom found;
- training is chiefly company-specific, and does not cover the comprehensive field required by the examinations; the potentials for apprentices to obtain qualifications through their participation in the production process is more left to chance and determined by the given work situation;
- training and work is coordinated locally and is strictly person-dependent; far less detailed and binding training plans are available than in industrial training; it would be very difficult to adhere to such binding plans;
- a characteristic feature of craftsmen training is the relatively frequent use of apprentices for non-training jobs, cleaning up and routine tasks;
- only part-time instructors are available; the master craftsman responsible for training being intensively involved with management tasks, usually transfers the actual training work to other members of the staff;
- qualifications in vocational theory are left exclusively to the vocational schools; workshop training is seldom to be found in craftsmen's training; the trainees consider this to be of low significance.

A relatively high number of trainees receive training in accordance with this modest qualification pattern in the Federal Republic of Germany: amounting to 34.9 % of all trainees (= crafts) in 1988, although agriculture (2.3 %) and retail sales trade have to be added, where training takes place along the same principles[72]. In order to compensate for the qualification deficits in this type of en-passant training, a comprehensive promotion programme for industry-wide vocational training establishments has been set up since the beginning of the seventies. The problems of this new place of learning are discussed at the end of the present chapter.

---

71 Mayer/Schumm, loc. cit., p. 62 ff. Fulda, W. et al: Berufsausbildung in Mittelbetrieben. Eine Untersuchung betrieblicher Lehr- und Lernprozesse, Alsbach 1994
72 Ditto, p. 55 ff.; Münch, J./H.-J. Müller et al: Interdependenz von Lernortkombinationen und Output-Qualitäten betrieblicher Berufsausbildug in ausgewählten Berufen, Berlin 1981

With regard to vocational qualifications for office and service vocations, companies are faced with problems basically different to those in industrial vocational training. The essential goal here is to go beyond the practical activities themselves and impart the capability to handle reference systems and interpret the information being dealt with (regarding persons, items or sectoral relationship) so that the sense of the actual job activity can also be understood[73].

In small and medium-sized industries and administrations this takes place in the form of a non-systematic type training for office and service vocations. Its characteristics are:

- in principle, training organisation is closely oriented to the company administration process; "learning by doing"; practical qualifications are obtained exclusively in this context;
- simultaneously, intensified theory training geared to reconstructing functional relationships which became lost due to the specialised division of labour;
- thus there is quite comprehensive school training (vocational school) with supporting company training on the one hand running parallel practical work on the job on the other and unconnected to training;
- part-time instructors; the mediator role of the non-professional training personnel is clearly determined by their work demand;
- local coordination of training and work; training and transfer plans are only generally structured; qualification deficits due to frequent elimination of special activities in organisations not concerned with production.

The systematic type of training for office and service vocations is of a higher quality and more or less comparable to industrial training in training workshops; it is mostly to be found in large companies and administrations. It differs from non-systematic training in the following main points:

- an attempt is made to overcome the separation of theory and practical training by additional organisational inputs; e. g. in-school and in-company training are linked through block and phase training;

---

73   Cf. Fluder-Ginesta, D.: Die Bürolehre. Eine Bestandsaufnahme, Aarau/Frankfurt a. M. 1984; Buck, B. (Publisher): Berufsbildung im Dienstleistungsbereich, Berlin/Bonn 1987

- longer training phases for theory separated from the company administration process; a high percentage of additional workshop training, training to obtain practice-oriented theoretical knowledge;

- central coordination of training and work; training and transfer plans with detailed timetable and organisational structuring;

- independent training department with full-time principal; full-time highly qualified instructors, training tutor in the individual departments of the company;

- trainees have the right of participation in training via direct participation in personnel selection and youth representation on the workers' council.

It becomes clear from the above attempt to typify the training systems that the quality of in-company training in the Federal Republic of Germany varies greatly – and this is a general characteristic of the dual training systems. The consequence is that trainees can be highly privileged or neglected. It has been proven, for example, that the quality of in-company training places clearly correlates to the level of general school leaving certificates obtained and the social origin of the trainees[74]. This intensification of unequal opportunities is far greater for in-school or purely market-oriented training systems. It is, therefore, stressed once again: the characteristic features of in-company training in the dual system of the Federal Republic of Germany are (1.) the existence of vocational trades which are formally equal and possessing a training monopoly, (2.) legally anchored training regulations and (3.) identically organized examinations, from the formal-legal viewpoint, which can be held exclusively by the Chambers.

However, this standardized training system has come under political pressure: In view of the very differing formal school-leaving certificates of the trainees compared to earlier times, it is suggested that a differentiation be made in the training courses field and certificates obtained: normal skilled-worker training for the majority, training for so-called ''weak learners'' below this qualification level, and elite training for young people possessing

---

74 Cf. Brandes, H./W. Brosi et al: Wege in die berufliche Bildung, in: Mitteilungen aus der Arbeitsmarkt- und Berufsforschung 19 (1986), 287- 297, p. 288 f.; Berufsbildungsbericht 1990, p. 37 ff.

the university entrance school-leaving certificate[75]. The attempt to implement such plans politically has been rejected initially although the educational policy pressure in this matter will no doubt remain[76].

3.2 The industry-wide vocational training establishment as a place of learning

The Vocational Training Act and the Trade Regulations Act do not put the decision regarding completeness of training in the hands of companies alone. Section 22 of the VTA and Section 23 of the HWO oblige companies who undertake or wish to undertake training but are not in a position fully to supply the prescribed training programme to arrange for supplementary training measures outside the place of training. Pursuant to Section 27 of the VTA, the training regulations can even stipulate the percentage of training to be carried out in other training centres. On the basis of this legal obligation of the companies, the Federal Government provided considerable funds as from the year 1973 to expand the capacity of industry-wide vocational training centres (Überbetriebliche Berufsbildungsstätte – ÜBS). In all, some DM 5.3 billion have been used to date to expand the ÜBS[77].

The main committee of the Federal Vocational Training Institute adopted a "catalogue of criteria for the evaluation of courses in industry-wide training centres"[78] which almost exactly reflects the terms of reference of this institution:

"Supplementary function for companies with specialised production, process and service structures in order to satisfy the requirements of the training regulations: compensation for regional disparities in training quality, widening of basic training, more in-depth and intensified specialised training, efficient achievement of learning goals fromthe training viewpoint

---

75 Berufsbildungsbericht 1989, p. 8
76 The announcement of a "paper on the promotion of gifted persons for vocational training" "Begabtenförderungswerk für die berufliche Bildung", cf. Informationen; Bildung, Wissenschaft, published by BMBW, 2/90, p. 10 f.
77 On the following cf. Beicht, U./J. Holzschuh et al: Strukturdaten überbetrieblicher Berufsausbildungsstätten 1984 (= Berichte zur beruflichen Bildung, No 93), Berlin/Bonn 1987
78 Ditto, p. 22 f.

- to systematise the flow of learning processes where this is not guaranteed in the company
- to satisfy the requirement that individual skills be practised and interconnected
- to break down complex tasks into simplified, model or simulated learning steps

More efficient achievement of learning goals from the economic viewpoint

- to avoid cost-intensive, accident-prone interventions in the work flow
- to achieve special learning goals in the training vocation which cannot be achieved in the individual companies
- to impart skills on cost-intensive facilities which would not run to full capacity at the macro-economic level

Adaptation to the technical, economic and social developments on the basis of training regulations.''

Industry-wide vocational training centres differ considerably from the other two places of learning in the dual system in regard to their sponsorship. Sponsors are primarily one or more commercial organisations, for example, chambers, guilds, the district craftsmen's associations, trade associations. In some instances the municipalities, districts, single or groups of companies also participate in sponsoring. In agriculture, the State Ministries or other State Authorities are usually sponsors. Industry-wide vocational training centres are hence neither school nor company. In the trade sector particularly, workshops in the vocational schools are used for industry-wide training. While these workshops are not industry-wide vocational training centres in the narrow sense, they should, however, be incorporated as facilities which are available for industry-wide training as a whole.

From the quantitative viewpoint, industry-wide vocational training centres can be broken down as follows, according to the most recent survey (1984):

Table 4: Number of industry-wide vocational training centres and workshop places according to training area

Training area	Training centre	Places
Manual trades	341	48,717
Industry/trade	85	10,191
Manual trades and industry/trade	19	5,136
Other	12	1,003
Total	457	65,047

Source: Beicht et al., Structural data on industry-wide vocational training centres 1984, Berlin/
Bonn 1987, page 46

Including those training centres under construction or in planning, a total of 70,794 workshop places were available in 1990. Thus the development goal of 77,100 workshop places which was laid down by the Federal-State-Commission for Educational Planning and Promotion of Research in the "old" Federal states has almost been achieved[79]. **Table 5** indicates the distribution of workshop places according to vocational trades.

In the case of the "new" Federal states the Federal Ministry for Education, Science, Research and Technology and the Federal Minister for Economic Affairs have designed harmonised programmes for the promotion of industry-wide vocational training centres. Since 1991 they have made available around DM 450m for this purpose. Following an initial promotional phase in which it was a matter of taking into account the most urgent needs, an efficient basic structure of industry-wide vocational training centres is to be established in a second phase which concentrates primarily on the regional economic centres.

The creation of industry-wide training centres marked a widely controversial vocational training policy program in the Federal Republic of Germany[80]. The Trade Unions complain primarily that the industry-wide vocational training centres are not subject to any public control despite the fact that their financing comes almost completely from the public sector.

---

79   Ditto, p 57 ff.

Table 5: Distribution of workshop places in industry-wide training centres according to vocational fields

Vocational fields	Workshop places	
	1984	under construction and in planning
Metalworking	25,183	2,882
Construction engineering	17,037	1,587
Electrical engineering	6,444	984
Timber engineering	4,424	419
Painting technology and interior decoration	2,728	371
Physical care	2,389	367
Nutrition and domestic science	2,236	346
Others	4,006	553
Total	64,447	7,509

Source: Beicht et al., loc. cit., pages 48 and 54

Furthermore – according to the Trade Unions – the industry-wide vocational training centres only partly (approximately 70 %) fulfilled their mandate – which was to supplement initial in-company training; they were increasingly being turned into further training centres and technology parks. Partly for reasons of costs the training companies refused to further expand industry-wide instruction, which meant that the industry-wide vocational training centres concentrated all the more on training master craftsmen and further training of self-employed master craftsmen[81]. The associations of

---

80   Cf. e.g. IG Metall: "Positionsbeschreibung zu den überbetrieblichen Ausbildungsstätten im Handwerk", (Frankfurt, no year of publication indicated); "Überbetriebliche Ausbildung – ein Faß ohne Boden?", Bericht über das Hearing des Auschusses für Bildung und Wissenschaft des Deutschen Bundestages vom 17.04.89, in: Die berufsbildende Schule 41 (1989), 403-408

81   IG Metall, loc. cit., however in the course of the programme of encouragement of the "new" Federal states the range of tasks of the industry-wide training centre has been officially expanded: according to the BMBW's guidelines on such encouragement, industry-wide training cetnres should always serve to provide supplementary vocational training and various measures of vocational further training (cf. Berufsbildungsbericht 1993, p. 121).

vocational training teachers criticized the fact that the industry-wide vocational training centres tended to become independent places of learning and, furthermore, were already becoming competitors to vocational schools. Due to the generous financing provided to industry-wide training centres, the vocational schools as public training facilities were evidently being rejected. The industry-wide vocational training centres were rolling headlong into becoming a type of "private vocational school system"[82].

We believe that these conflicts clearly demonstrate that the relationship between places of learning in the dual system of the Federal Republic of Germany has lost its balance and should be recoordinated[83]. It should be clear, however, that this recoordination must take place between three and not two places of learning. Indications of a shift in emphasis in the three places of learning can already be observed in the "new" Federal states within the context of the promotion of industry-wide vocational training centres. In the course of the reconstruction of a medium-sized private sector the vocational training centres here largely take on the role of a central instrument for securing "new blood" in small and medium-sized businesses (cf. Vocational Training Act 1992, p. 163).

3.3 The vocational school as the place of learning

The conference of Education Ministers defined vocational schools as "schools to be attended by persons subject to compulsory vocational training or those entitled to vocational training, who are undergoing their initial vocational training or have entered into a work relationship... Training is given on a part-time basis on one or several days of the week or in connected subsegments (block training); it is closely related to in-plant training, including training in industry-wide training centres. Within the scope of vocational training, which is broken down into initial and specialised stages, the initial stage can take the form of a basic vocational training year with full-time one-year training, or be organised cooperatively within the dual system"[84]. Attendance at a vocational school is generally compulsory for

---

82 Die berufsbildende Schule, loc. cit., p. 404
83 Cf. Greinert, W.-D.: Auf dem Wege zum Marktmodell? – Bemerkungen zur heraufziehenden Krise der dualen Berufsausbildung in der Bundesrepublik, in: Harney, K./G. Pätzold (Publisher): Arbeit und Ausbildung. Wissenschaft und Politik, Frankfurt a.M. 1990, p. 275 – 288.
84 Bezeichnungen zur Gliederung des beruflichen Schulwesens, Beschluß der KMK vom 8.12.1975

all young people not attending higher or vocational full-time schools up until their 18th birthday or until they have completed their vocational training. Attendance at vocational school is no longer compulsory after reaching 21 years of age. This compulsory vocational schooling is anchored in the schooling legislation of the individual Federal States.

The Youth Labour Protection Act (Jugendarbeitsschutzgesetz – JArbSchG) containsregulations concerning the leave of the trainees and juvenile workers. Section 9 stipulates:

''(1) The employer is to provide leave of absence for the juveniles to participate in training at the vocational school. He may not employ juveniles

1. before training when this commences at 9 o'clock.
2. in a vocational school day consisting of more than five training lessons lasting at least 45 minutes each, once per week.
3. in vocational school weeks with a scheduled block training of at least 25 hours, for at least five days; additional in-plant training events of up two hours a week are admissible.''

The facilities and differentiation of courses at vocational schools are largely geared to the economic structure of the given region, i.e. the structure of training places offered in the region is reflected in the specialisation courses provided at the vocational school. The vocational schools specialise along the following lines:

– industrial-technical vocational schools,
– commercial-administrative vocational schools,
– domestic science-nursing vocational schools,
– agricultural vocational schools and
– mining vocational schools[85].

The forms of organisation of these vocational schools, which are financed by the Municipality or District Authority (equipment and material costs) and the Federal States (personnel costs), can be directly derived from this structuring. A division is made into

---

85   Cf. Lipsmeier, A.: Organisation und Lernorte der Berufsausbildung, Munich 1978, p. 122

- schools oriented to vocational groupings in large cities and in industrial agglomerations (e.g.vocational schools for electrical engineering);
- schools geared to specific sectors of the economy in medium-sized towns (e.g. industrial vocational schools, commercial vocational schools etc.);
- schools covering several sectors of the economy in a Rural District Authority or cooperative vocational schools (e.g. vocational schools in a given district).

Structures geared to specific vocational fields are gaining in predominance, particularly in large cities and agglomerations when organizing new schools. The breakdown into vocational fields commenced with the establishment of the basic vocational training year. In terms of specialisation and content, the vocational field encompasses an ensemble of common basic skills and knowledge which provide the foundation for access to a number of related training courses in the more specialised courses of vocational training[86]. As the basic vocational training year is the basic stage of the vocational training from a legal and organisational point of view, it is expedient to apply this structuring principle consistently to the entire organisation of vocational schools[87]. For so-called ''splinter'' vocations, i.e. training vocations for which only a small number of persons are trained, centralised vocational schooling is offered at district or state level or even on a nationwide basis (e. g. the Specialised District Class for road builders).

Pursuant to the resolution of the Committee of Education Ministers of 1975, already mentioned above, vocational schools have the task of teaching people the general and specialised subjects, with particular attention to the requirements of vocational training. 8 to 16 lessons per week are provided in these schools, but it should be noted that, although guaranteed officially and by law, the number of lessons varies greatly depending on the type of school and the region. Bottlenecks in school developments, particularly concerning the supply of teachers, even nowadays continues to hinder the prescribed number of training lessons from being provided in full[88]. In 1986, for example, 353,873 of 1.972 million students of vocation-

---

86 Holz, H./E. Ladewig et al: Berufsgrundbildung: Daten, Aspekte, Modellversuche, Hanover 1974, p. 89 f.
87 Cf. for example, the principle of the ''Oberstufenzentren'' in Berlin, which are rigorously structured and named in accordance with the vocational fields.

al schools received less than 8 lessons, 309,688 received 8 lessons; the remainder received 9 lessons and more or even full-time training (BGJ, BVJ).

Table 6 illustrates some of the major structural data in the period 1980-1988. It is evident that considerable successes have been achieved, for example, in reducing the size of classes, in professionalising teaching, in improving the teacher-student ratio and the provision of instruction. Nevertheless, in view of the specific developments vocational schools face great problems, particularly in regard to assuring that their teaching is up to date and comprehensive.

---

88 Cf. regarding the figures: Fachserie 11, Bildung und Kultur, Reihe 2, Berufliche Schulen, 1986, published by Statistischen Bundesamt Wiesbaden, p. 49; zur Berufsschulsituation heute Cf. Davids, S.: Die Berufsschule in Urteil von Auszubildenden und Ausbildern (= Berichte zur beruflichen Bildung, No 100), Berlin/Bonn 1988; Max-Traeger-Stiftung (Publisher): Berufsbildung im Wandel. Neue Aufgaben für die Berufsschule. MTS-Script Nr. 3, (Frankfurt 1988). An älteren Untersuchungen Cf. Crusius, R.: Der Lehrling in der Berufsschule, Munich 1973

Table 6: Statistical structural data for vocational schooling 1980 – 1988

	1980	1984	1986	1987	1988
Vocational schools	1583	1711	1512	1485	1492
Students (1,000s)	1847.5	1858.3	1857.2	1773.1	1674.2
– with training contract %	92.7	96.0	96.7	96.1	96.5
– foreign students %	3.8	4.1	4.5	5.1	5.9
Previous schooling (%)					
– without lower school leaving cert.	10.0	6.9	6.4	6.0	6.0
– lower school leaving cert.	54.0	45.8	40.9	40.4	39.3
– intermediate school leaving cert.	31.9	38.3	41.3	42.0	42.1
– university/college entrance qualification	4.1	9.0	11.4	11.5	12.5
Classes	79743	83947	83807	81713	78794
Teaching per week (lessons)	9.1	10.2	10.9	11.0	–
– up to 8 lessons (% of class)	47.9	41.0	38.6	37.0	35.0
– 9 to 12+ lessons (%)	34.2	39.5	42.5	45.9	48.9
– block teaching (%)	17.6	16.8	16.2	16.3	15.3
Students per class	23.3	22.1	22.2	21.7	21.2
Teachers					
– main job	32560	36881	39892	40005	–
– secondary job	18996	17741	11786	10604	–
Students per teacher	–	51.7	48.7	48.1	45.4
Weekly teaching (1,000 lessons)	723.0	859.3	911.5	897.5	–
– main job teachers (%)	85.1	88.8	93.1	93.7	–
– secondary job teachers (%)	14.9	11.2	6.9	6.3	–

Source: Vocational Training Report 1990, page 97

The instruction, averaging eleven lessons per week, covers approximately 6-8 lessons of vocation-related instruction (e. g. technology, technical mathematics, technical drawing for industrial trades) and three lessons in general subjects (German, politics, economics). Religious instruction is also usually provided and, in a very few cases, sport[89]. In practice, the focus is clearly placed on vocation-related subjects because the other subjects in the vocational school curriculum are not significant for the final examination. Pursuant to Section 35 of the VTA, the instruction in the vocational school is only relevant for examination "to the extent that it provides subject matter which is essential for the vocational training".

For a long time the part-time vocational school provided no certificate of training, i.e. it was a "training cul-de-sac". This has now changed: since 1979 the vocational school can also award lower school-leaving certificates in all Federal States: furthermore Berlin, Baden-Württemberg and North-Rhine-Westphalia recognize the vocational school certificate (including the final vocational examination) as an intermediate school-leaving certificate when specific requirements are fulfilled[90]. In this way, the vocational school has achieved an initial link with the general certification system of general schools.

A principle problem of vocational schools which has been pinpointed is the coordination of organisational structure and curriculum with those of the in-company place of learning. In the past, repeated efforts have been made to blend more closely practical, in-company training and theory qualifications in the vocational school, where the vocational schools have always played the "reacting" role. It was hoped that the situation would be relieved especially by consistently applying the system of specialised classes (= upgraded mono-vocational classes) and a specific didactic concept for training in vocational schools[91]. As only limited success was achieved from these efforts, further activities were undertaken at the beginning of the sev-

---

89 Lipsmeier, loc. cit., p. 127 f.
90 Pampus, K.: Die Verbindung beruflicher Qualifikationen mit allgemeinen Schulabschlüssen, special publication by the BiBB, Berlin 1981
91 In particular, the didactic discussion on the upstream-, downstream- or parallel principle should be mentioned; Cf. Grüner, G.: Bausteine zur Berufsschuldidaktik, Trier 1978, particularly p. 135 ff.

enties for better coordination of places of learning. The Coordination Procedure for Training Regulations and Guideline Curricula agreed between the Federal Government and the Ministries of Education of the individual stage should be mentioned first of all[92], together with more intensified block training, which was intended to align the organisation of learning[93]. The attempt to enforce a basic vocational training year was linked with intentions for much further-reaching reform. According to the Vocational Training Act, the aim of vocational training was to impart ''wide basic vocational training and the specialized skills and knowledge required to exercise a qualified trade, within the scope of orderly training courses'' (Section 1, 2). Basic vocational training was thus practically given the status of a legally-binding component of vocational training, and training regulations are nowadays being specifically designed to fulfil this obligation[94]. In addition to such decisions based on qualification theory, other arguments were used at the beginning of the seventies to support the introduction of general basic vocational training:

– pedagogic and development psychological arguments expansion of the school as a 'protected' area, gradually guiding young people to make a well-founded vocational choice;
– educational policy arguments: balancing of regional and sectoral inequalities with regard to opportunities for vocational training; creation of an intermediate educational certificate for working youth;
– socio-political arguments: expansion of capacity in the training offered; preventive employment security[95].

The basic vocational training year (BGJ) was first introduced at the beginning of the seventies, with two main options: full-time schooling (BGJ/s) and the cooperative form (BGJ/k). The vocational training year as full-time schooling is an institution of the public educational system under the super-

---

92 Cf. ''Gemeinsames Ergebnisprotokoll betreffend das Verfahren bei der Abstimmung von Ausbildungsordnungen und Rahmenlehrplänen im Bereich der beruflichen Bildung'', of 30.05.1972
93 Cf. Franke, G./M. Kleinschmitt: Das Blocksystem in der dualen Berufsausbildung, (= Berichte zur beruflichen Bildung, No 19) Berlin 1979; Müller, I.: Der Blockunterricht im Urteil von Schülern, Munich 1980
94 Cf. the reorganised metal and electrical trades, which provide for a general phase of basic vocational trainining.
95 Cf. Greinert, W.-D./D. Jungk (Publisher): Berufliche Grundbildung, Frankfurt a. M./New York 1982, p. 10 ff.

vision of the education ministers of the individual states. From the viewpoint of educational law, the BGJ/s basic vocational year is a full-time form of vocational schooling which replaces the first year of in-plant and in-school vocational training. In the BGJ/s both general subjects and vocational training theory are taught together with practical basic vocational skills in the school. In the cooperative type of basic vocational training year (BGJ/k) the companies and schools work together in the dual system. The students have training contracts and receive their practical vocational training in the company and vocational theory and general education in the school. School training is extended to 2 to 2½ days per week.

The organisation and operation of the BGJ and it training policy siting are regulated by:

- the regulation concerning the creditation of the basic vocational training year dated 17.6.1978[96] and
- the general agreement on the basic vocational training year of the Conference of the Ministry of Education (KMK) dated 19.5.1978 [97].

Referring to Section 29, 1 of the VTA, the regulation concerning creditation stipulates that training in the basic vocational training year counts fully towards a subsequent vocational training in the dual system. For this, it is necessary to stipulate the number of lessons in vocation-field related training (vocational practice and vocational theory) and also the training vocations in which the attendance at a basic vocational training year has to be fully credited.

The vocational field, defined as ''an aggregate of common basic vocational skills and knowledge which constitute the basis for access to a number of related training courses in the more specialised phases of vocational training'', is the basic organisational principle and framework for determining subject contents in the basic vocational year[98].

Vocational fields during the basic vocational training year:
I   Business and administration

---

96   Federal Law Gazette I, p. 1061 ff.
97   Beschlüsse der KMK. Berufliche Bildung, Neuwied (Luchterhand), Gruppe 6.0, 6.1 - 6.13
98   Cf. Footnote 86

II	Metalworking
III	Electrical engineering
IV	Construction engineering
V	Timber engineering
VI	Textile engineering and clothing
VII	Chemistry, physics and biology
VIII	Printing technology
IX	Painting technology and interior decoration
X	Health
XI	Physical care
XII	Nutrition and domestic science
XIII	Agriculture

The general agreement regulates the admission requirements, teaching, and the leaving certificates for the basic vocational training year, whereby the chief provisions concern the learning goals and learning contents in vocational theory and vocational practice.

Table 7 indicates the quantitative development path of the basic vocational training year since 1980. It becomes evident on the one hand, that the development of the basic vocational training year depends on the market situation for training places. As the training market becomes strained, the number of students in the basic vocational training year increases; with the relaxation on the market as from 1984/85, the number of the students attending the – voluntary – in-school basic vocational training year reduced drastically. On the other hand, the table indicates a large increase in students attending the cooperative basic training year. In 1990 there was a shift in the quantitative relationship between full-time schooling and cooperative basic vocational training years. This development is probably due mainly to the entry into force of the new training schemes which prescribe almost universally a basic training across vocational fields in the first year[99].

---

99   Cf. Footnote 65; more recent data on BGJ, cf. Berufsbildungsbericht 1994, p. 75 f.

Table 7: Students in the basic vocational training year 1980-1992 (thousands)

Year	Schooling type	Cooperative type
1980	66.1	14.4
1981	80.0	16.6
1982	86.1	17.3
1983	88.4	18.8
1984	87.1	17.9
1985	80.1	15.5
1986	68.9	18.2
1987	58.8	28.2
1988	50.1	37.2
1989	41.3	39.7
1990	36.6	47.0
1991*	34.6	53.7
1992*	31.3	49.2

* Germany as a whole; previously "old" Federal states

Source: Basic and structural data 1993/94, p.40

Overall it can be said that the BGJ-program of the early seventies, which intended to introduce this educational institution generally as a replacement for the first year of training, has failed. Although the cooperative BGJ is expanding in the course of the restructuring of training vocations, and although for reasons of the relevant costs the employers' associations are now pushing some of the Federal states to take over their BGJ programmes which have come to a halt, the opportunity for modernisation of the dual system through the introduction of a general compulsory basic training specific to vocational fields has probably been wasted. This is particularly true of the vocational school, which as the institution principally responsible for matters of basic training could have found a new extensive role now that the separation of theory and practice into specific centres of learning is beginning to become increasingly obsolete.

4 Vocational training outside the dual system

If we do not consider vocational training at the academic level, in-school vocational training in the Federal Republic of Germany from the viewpoint of initial training takes place – institutionally – only in the specialised vocational trade schools (Berufsfachschule – BFS).

4.1 The vocational trade schools (Berufsfachschulen) in the Federal Republic of Germany

According to the definition of the Standing Conference of Ministers of Education, Berufsfachschulen are ''schools offering full-time courses with a minimum of one-year attendance and not requiring any previous vocational training or vocational activity as entrance qualification. Their task is to teach general and vocational subjects and to provide students with the capability to obtain a certificate in a recognized training vocation or in one section of vocational training in one or several recognized training vocations, or to allow him/her to obtain a vocational training certificate which can only be obtained in schools''[100].

According to this definition we can categorize three types of Berufsfachschulen (vocational trade schools);

Type 1:
Berufsfachschulen which offer certificates in recognized training vocations;

Type 2:
Berufsfachschulen offering vocational training organized exclusively in schools;

Type 3:
Berufsfachschulen at which attendance counts towards training time in recognized training vocations.

---

100 Bezeichnungen zur Gliederung des beruflichen Schulwesens; Beschluß der Kultusministerkonferenz vom 8.12.1975

Berufsfachschulen of Type 1 and 2 are seldom found; for example there are probably less than 20,000 training places in Type 1 schools[101]. This type of school partly dates back to the 19th century; they were originally established to train the elite workers (works master craftsmen). Berufsfachschulen awarding full qualifications (abbreviation BFS q) between 1975-1985 had the prime function of being nets to catch young people who did not have an apprenticeship contract, even though they did award higher school-leaving certificates (e. g. the Fachhochschulreife (university entrance qualification restricted to a specified field of study). The BFS q for vocations concerning artistic craft are still distinctly schools for training the elite. These schools for precious metalworking, wood carving, basket-making, violin-making, ceramics/glass and graphic arts also have a long tradition and, nowadays attended by young people with an intermediary or higher school-leaving certificate, are, therefore, a type of "school of vocational arts" for this special clientele[102].

In the Berufsfachschule Type 2, the so-called "higher Berufsfachschule" is the dominating type offering training in so-called assistant vocations. The entrance qualification for training is the intermediate school leaving certificate. Training generally covers a period of two years. In the Federal Republic of Germany 'assistant' vocations are generally found in the field of technology (23 different specialisations: chemical-technical laboratory assistant through to technical assistant for design and production technology) and in health care (10 subject areas: from medico-technologist for radiology, pharmaceutical-laboratory assistant etc.), they are so-called "school vocations" i.e. not training vocations in the scope of the dual vocational training system[103].

The Berufsfachschule Type 3 provides by far the highest amount of training. It can be attended after completion of 9th grade of the secondary school and covers two-year (in most cases) or one-year courses. The one-year Berufsfachschulen are nowadays considered, both from the legal and statistical viewpoint, as an integral component of the dual system. 13 subject

---

101 Cf. Grüner, G.: Die beruflichen Vollzeitschulen – eine Alternative zum dualen System, in: Lipsmeier, A. (Publisher): Berufsbildungspolitik in den 70er Jahren, Wiesbaden 1983, 123-133, p. 130
102 Ditto, p. 129 f
103 Ditto, p. 130 f.

areas are presently covered: commerce, metalworking, electrical engineering, automotive engineering, industrial drawing, building/timber, textiles and clothing, leather, chemistry/physics/biology, printing and paper, graphics and photography, hotel and catering, nutrition and catering. The certificate obtained after a two-year BFS-course is equivalent to the intermediate school-leaving certificate from a Realschule; these are schools with "extended learning goals". The successful attendance at a one-year and two-year Berufsfachschule-course can be credited as one to one-and-a-half-years towards the training time in a recognized training vocation, depending on the amount of vocational training given[104].

This legal obligation to recognize the course of study toward a later training satisfies the expectations of many young people: they consider the Berufsfachschule to be a 'through-station' or a place to receive basic vocational training.

Table 8: Students in Berufsfachschulen (1960-1982) in thousand

Year	total	of which female
1960	125.7	88.5
1965	148.5	96.5
1970	182.7	112.6
1975	270.8	182.4
1980	325.6	223.7
1982	356.3	245.9
1984	347.2	243.8
1986	318.7	219.4
1988	285.3	189.2
1990	245.6	157.2
1991*	239.2	154.0
1992*	253.2	164.2

Source: BMBW: Basic and structural data 1993/1994, pages 40 and 48

---

104 Cf. Corresponding Berufsgrundbildungsjahr-Anrechnungs-Verordnungen vom 17. Juli 1978 (Federal Law Gazette I, p. 1061), 20. Juli 1979 (Federal Law Gazette I, p. 1142), 20. Juni 1980 (Federal Law Gazette p. 738), 2. Juli 1980 (Federal Law Gazette I, p. 827), 10. März 1988 (BGBl I, p. 229), 31. Mai 1988 (Federal Law Gazette I, p. 719) and Berufsfachschul-Anrechnungs-Verordnung vom 22. Juni 1973 (Federal Law Gazette I, p. 665)

The latest survey of students from the Berufsfachschule (1989) indicated that 44 % of the graduates of the one- and two-year BFS-courses intended to commence a shortened training in a training vocation, i.e. to transfer to the dual vocational training system[105]. This percentage was far higher in the seventies (approximately 70 %) when many young people used the Berufs-fachschule as a "waiting room" because of the shortage of apprenticeship posts.

As indicated in Table 8, the training volume of all Berufsfachschulen (the one-year-courses are not included!) has greatly increased over the last 20 years, reaching its peak in 1983 (356,700 students). In view of the lower demand for apprenticeship posts and the growing absorptive capacity of the dual system this expansion has decreased since 1984; according to esti-mates by the KMK, the number of students at Berufsfachschulen is expect-ed to drop further[106]. The other so-called "vocational schools" in the Fed-eral Republic of Germany, with the exception of the Fachschule, are educational institutions which chiefly award school certificates but do not offer vocational training. These include particularly the Berufsaufbauschu-len, Fachoberschulen and berufliche Gymnasien[107]. These schools are gen-erally organised in vocational training centres together with Berufsschulen and Berufsfachschulen.

4.2 Vocational further training in the Federal Republic of Germany

Vocational training in the narrower sense covers both initial vocational training and further vocational training. This training area is relatively dif-ficult to define in the Federal Republic of Germany, due not least to the fact that it is characterised by the market model. An exact definition is rendered all the more difficult because competing terms such as 'vocational adult ed-ucation' and 'vocational continued training' are also often used. We con-

---

105 Berufsbildungsbericht 1990, p. 50
106 Whether the increase in 1992 continues to indicate an increasing tendency to attend vocation-al trade schools following the expansion of this type of school in the "new" Federal states remains to be seen.
107 Cf. Bezeichnungen zur Gliederung des beruflichen Schulwesens (8.12.1975), Anhang; zusammenfassend: Stratmann, K.: Stufen der Berufsbildung, in: Müllges, U. (Publisher): Handbuch der Berufs- und Wirtschaftspädagogik, Bd. 2, Düsseldorf 1979, p. 279-347

sider further vocational training to cover "all organised, and consequently institutionalised, learning processes" which are the continuation of a formal training course (e. g. in the dual system) or immediately connect to a professional qualification obtained through long years of work experience, and intend to provide further vocational training of any form or purpose[108].

Further vocational training in the Federal Republic of Germany can, therefore, be broken down into the following forms:

1. Further vocational training in the narrower sense

– pursuant to the Vocational Training Act (defined here as "further vocational training") in companies and in extra-company establishments
– outside the regulations of the Vocational Training Act in companies and extra-company establishments
– pursuant to the educational laws of the States in vocational schools (universities and technical colleges do not fall into the category of further vocational training!)
– pursuant to the adults-(further-)educational legislation of the States, in adult evening classes and other establishments
– pursuant to the Civil Servants Act in academies and internal civil service courses

2. Retraining

– in special retraining centres
– in companies, commissioned by the Labour Office

3. Vocational rehabilitation

– in vocational training centres

4. Vocational reactivation

– in companies
– in retraining and vocational training centres.

---

108 Cf. Münch, J.: Das berufliche Bildungswesen in der Bundesrepublik Deutschland, 3rd edn. Luxemburg 1987, p. 205; the following classification of vocational further training is also based on Münch's remarks.

The Vocational Training Act (VTA) which essentially regulates initial vocational training, also contains stipulations governing further vocational training. Under Section 1, 3 of the VTA a differentiation can be made between adaptive further vocational training and further education leading to upward mobility. Further education measures leading to upward mobility aim to prepare participants to sit an examination. Upon successfully passing the examination they obtain a certificate, which documents the higher vocational qualification. Part of these measures prepare the students for examinations in recognized further training vocations (e. g. technician, master craftsmen, etc.), another part is geared to company or branch internal qualifications. Adaptive further training chiefly aims to supplement existing knowledge and skills in order to satisfy the current requirements of the job involved. Adaptive further training measures usually cover a relatively short period of time[109].

Companies are the chief sponsors of vocational further training; however, educational institutes of the Chambers of Industry and Commerce, of the craft trades, the Vocational Training Centre of the German Trade Union Association (DGB) and the German Salaried Workers Union (DAG) and the numerous educational foundations in the private sector are engaged in further vocational training[110] Pursuant to Section 46 of the VTA, the Chambers can hold examinations as evidence of the qualifications obtained from further vocational training. The Federal Minister for Education, Science, Research and Technology also has the right to decree legal regulations on the implementation of examinations in the field of further vocational training, in agreement with the competent specialised ministries. These refer exclusively to further education leading to upward mobility.

In addition to further vocational training implemented pursuant to the VTA, in accordance with the regulations of the Federation and the Chambers, and leading to recognized qualifications, numerous other vocational training courses are offered – mostly at company level – which exclusively provide adaptive training, and do not generally lead to formal qualifica-

---

109 Der Bundesminister für Bildung und Wissenschaft (Publisher): Stand und Perspektiven der beruflichen Weiterbildung in der Bundesrepublik Deutschland (= Studien zu Bildung und Wissenschaft 1), Bad Honnef 1984, p. 156 f.; a current summary is provided by "Berichtssystem Weiterbildung 1991" (integrated overall report on the further training situation in the old and new Federal states, published by BMBW), Bonn 1993.
110 Cf. Voigt, W.: Berufliche Weiterbildung. Eine Einführung, Munich 1986, p. 14 ff. and 23 ff.

tions. To date it has been difficult to assess the volume of these educational measures outside the regulations of the VTA[111]. According to the "1991 Reporting System on Further Education"[112] published recently, in 1992, 21 % of Germans between the ages of 19 and 64 attended vocational further training courses. Extrapolated this amounts to 9.8m attending at a national level, 2.5m of these in the "new" Federal states. This figure is markedly greater than the orders of magnitude shown previously in other statistics.

In the wide spectrum of vocation-related further training the most socialized type is the Fachschule (specialized school). The entrance requirements to these schools comprise a successfully completed vocational training course or corresponding practical employment in the vocation, plus further professional experience. Although they can be sponsored by many different sources, ranging from state to private organisations, the specialised schools have a very similar typology (long-term training offer, theory courses, systematic learning), because their certificates are state recognized.

At the present time some 210,000 people are attending courses in specialized schools, concentrating on the following subject areas: technology (certificate state examined technician), business economics, agriculture, home economics, social pedagogics, design, geriatrics, foreign languages; the numerous specialised schools for the craft trades which prepare journeymen for their master craftsmen examination[113].

During the seventies, laws covering adult education and educational leave were adopted in most of the Federal States; these were particularly designed to support general and political education for adults (earners). These further training measures are primarily sponsored by the Adult Educational Centres (Volkshochschulen – VHS) which offer an increasing number of courses for further vocational training. From the quantitative viewpoint, some 20 % of the courses offered by the VHS adult education centres (there are 1,000 VHS with 4,000 field centres in Germany) can be categorised as

---

111 Cf. Wittwer, W.: Weiterbildung im Betrieb – Darstellung und Analyse, Munich 1982; Bardeleben, R. V. et al: Strukturen betrieblicher Weiterbildung (= Berichte zur beruflichen Bildung, No 83), Berlin/Bonn 1986
112 Cf. "Berichtssystem Weiterbildung", loc. cit., p. 42
113 Cf. Voigt, loc. cit., p. 26 ff.

vocational further training, concentrating on the commercial-administrative sector. The courses offered reach some 360,000 -400,000 people[114].

Each year some 300,000 people take part in seminars and courses for vocational retraining. Retraining measures aim to "allow transfer into another, suitable vocational activity"[115]. The courses can either teach new activities or provide two- to three-year- training in a recognized training vocation.

"Vocational rehabilitation" covers all medical, training and social measures which aim to integrate handicapped persons, sick people and people suffering from the consequences of accidents into professional life[116]. Some 3.3 to 4.3 million handicapped persons live in the Federal Republic of Germany. 25 rehabilitation centres with approx 12,500 places plus 8,000 places in other establishments are available to these people for further training and retraining measures. Vocational rehabilitation measures only focus on a few vocations in the technical and commercial-administrative sector[117].

Vocational reactivation is an area of further vocational training which has only been slightly institutionalised to date. The aim is to impart or update vocational knowledge and skills which have been forgotten or become outdated due to long interruptions to working life. This sector of further vocational training is particularly significant for women wishing to return to their old or new vocation after an absence from work for family reasons.

Further vocational training in the Federal Republic of Germany has become particularly significant since the adoption of the Labour Support Act (Arbeitsförderungsgesetz – AFG) in 1969 and has considerably expanded since this time. This law was originally intended as an instrument for active qualification and labour market policy: the level of vocational performance was to be raised, the structures of vocations and the provision of equal opportunities was to be improved, technical and economic progress was to be

114 Cf. Pflüger, A.: Berufliche Weiterbildung an Volkshochschulen (= Päd. Arbeitsstelle des DVV), Frankfurt a.M., no year of publication indicated
115 Cf. Voigt, loc. cit., p. 15
116 Der Bundesminister für Bildung und Wissenschaft, loc. cit., p. 158; Podeszta, H. et al: Die berufliche Rehabilitation behinderter Erwachsener (= Berichte zur Berufsbildung, No 73), Berlin/Bonn 1985
117 Voigt, loc. cit., p. 16

advanced. However since the mid-1970s the funds available under the Labour Support Act have chiefly been used to control unemployment and provide further vocational training for the unemployed[118]. Pursuant to Section 50, paragraph 1 of the Labour Support Act, the Federal Labour Office can "grant loans and subsidies for the development, expansion and equipment of facilities, including industry-wide training workshops, which serve to advance vocational training, further education or retraining". In specific cases, funds under the Labour Support Act can also be used to finance the ongoing operations of such establishments. This "institutional support" is supplemented by "individual support" used to provide personal support to persons participating in training measures.

Practically all areas and sponsors of further vocational training have benefited from the funds made available through the Labour Support Act, not least numerous so-called "free sponsors" and commercial enterprises, established specifically to implement further professional education. A continuous increase in the number of persons supported via the Labour Support Act has been ascertained since 1980. This expansion is due to two main factors:

1. The current mass unemployment, and
2. the collapse of the East German economy after 1989. In 1992, 574,700 people (43 % of them women) had joined a scheme in the "old" Federal states. Of these people, 62.6 % were unemployed prior to joining, including around a fifth long-term unemployed. In the "new" Federal states 887,555 people had begun a further training course in 1992, 62 % of them women[119].

The list of sponsors is headed by companies, who provide more than 44 % of all further training courses. Way behind them are private institutions, professional associations and academies or (technical) universities. These are in turn followed by chambers, adult education centres, trades unions, technical colleges and the employers' associations[120].

---

118 Ditto, p. 18 ff.
119 Berufsbildungsbericht 1994, p. 127
120 Berichtssystem Weiterbildung, loc. cit., p. 240; although the list contains further-training sponsors which we would not include under this category, it nevertheless underlines the dominating position of the companies, which has been further developed since then.

It can be summarized that, as we have indicated, the vocational training sector not covered by the dual system does not provide a uniform picture. The dual system clearly predominates in the field of initial vocational training (1992: 1,666,600 trainees); vocational training in schools can be considered as a negligible remainder, particularly when considering that half of the approximately 250,000 students in Berufsfachschulen continue their vocational training in the dual system after completing the in-school course.

Vocational further training presents quite a different picture: there are 1.66 million trainees in the dual system compared with some 9.8 million "in further education"[121]. This comparison must, of course, take into account the fact that while initial vocational training has a throughput time of 3-3½ years, that required for further training is low to very low - for example, just the time required for operational induction. However, if the comparison is continued on the basis of funding inputs it becomes evident that numerous companies nowadays spend three to four times the amounton further vocational training than on initial vocational training. Unfortunately the available data does not allow further information on this aspect[122].

---

121 Berichtssystem Weiterbildung, loc. cit., p. 42
122 Cf. Grund- und Strukturdaten 1993/94, p. 264; the percentage for vocational further training cannot be estimated.

5 Functional analysis of the German training system

The dual system of vocational training in the Federal Republic of Germany "no matter how excellent it was in earlier times, no longer satisfies the requirements of a modern industrial society"[123]. Experience from the last 15 years indicates that this harsh judgement by the OECD from the year 1973 can be rated as a clear misjudgement. Only a small amount of data from the "vocational training report 1990" of the Federal Government has to be put forward in order to arrive as a completely opposite judgement: some 1.3 million young people were undergoing dual training at the beginning of the seventies, with the number rising to 1.8 million by the mid-eighties; at the beginning of the seventies some 50 % of an age group between 16 and 19 completed vocational training organised in the dual system, whilst the figure was 75 % in 1990; the training quota (number of trainees per hundred employees) has risen from just on 6 % in the mid-1960s to over 8 % in 1988; whereas the number of 40-50 year old adults who had not completed vocational training still accounted for approx. 27 %, it has fallen to 13 % of the 20-30 year olds from high-birth-rate years; 90 % of young people entering working life nowadays hold vocational training or university qualifications[124]. This means that, despite the high birth rate years and a growing number of young foreigners reaching training age, the quota of non-skilled workers has decreased by 50 % since the beginning of the seventies.

5.1 Basis of the functional analysis

Vocational training systems are systems of social behaviour. In the perspective of modern system theory they mark a "meaning context of social actions ... which refer to each other and can be defined by an environment of unrelated actions"[125].

---

123 OECD: Bildungswesen: mangelhaft. BRD-Bildungspolitik im OECD-Länderexamen, published by K. Hüfner, Frankfurt 1973
124 Berufsbildungsbericht 1990, p. 1
125 Cf. Luhmann, N.: Soziologie als Theorie sozialer Systeme, in: the same: Soziologische Aufklärung 1. Aufsätze zur Theorie sozialer Systeme, Opladen 1970, 113 – 139, p. 115

In contrast to older theories[126], this viewpoint – system boundaries as meaning boundaries – identifies the point of reference of social systems outside the system, namely in the problem which the system is supposed to solve for its environment. The relationships between the system and the overall social system are here termed *function*, the relationships between the system and other systems *performance*, and the relationships of the system with itself *reflection*.

If we follow the analysis categories of this "functional-structural" approach (which is particularly associated with the name of Niklas Luhmann) the system of vocational training may be understood as a meaning relationship of actions (or of communication) which differentiates itself from other meanings by reference to a particular social problem and has defined itself by its environment. The process whereby the system of vocational training found its identity occurred at the point when the system set about proving itself as definably functional for a differentiated social problem. Since this time "vocational training" as a social behavioural system and reflection category has demanded a certain singularity in respect of its problem-solving capacity: the imminent problem, so it was claimed, could not be solved – or at least not solved better – by any other social behavioural system[127].

So what is now the problem which was or is to be solved for society by means of the system of vocational training?

If we look at Germany as an example, this question cannot be answered in a single sentence since the social behavioural system of vocational training has accumulated solution capacities for various problems in the course of its development process which today play an important part in its highly complex structure[128]. To describe this process here even in outline would be too wide a field, so we must satisfy ourselves with resorting to the function(s) of the so-called "dual" training system as shown by current vocational training research for its developed form. In this way, the following original functions of the vocational training system can be identified[129]:

126 Cf. e.g. Parsons, T.: An Outline of Social System, in: the same: Theories of Society, New York 1961, 30-79; Buckley, W.: Society as a complex adaptive System, in: the same (Publisher): Modern System Research for the Behavioral Scientist, Chicago 1968, 490-513
127 Cf. Luhmann, N./K.-E. Schorr: Reflexionsprobleme im Erziehungssystem, Stuttgart 1979
128 Cf. Greinert, W.-D.: The "German System" of Vocational Education. Hystory, Organization, Prospects, Baden-Baden 1993

- the qualification function,
- the allocation function,
- the selection and status distribution function,
- the absorption and preservation function,
- the utilisation function and
- the integration function (socialisation, legitimation function).

These terms need to be explained in more detail. In outline, a vocational training system must

1. be capable of satisfying the qualification needs of the employment system. Since the term qualification is generally abstracted from the qualitative differences of the requirement for specialist staff, the term allocation serves for this purpose,
2. differentiate the needs of the employment system according to type and level of vocational requirements. A vocational training system must moreover
3. regulate access to the various privileged training courses, vocations and professional positions, i.e. it essentially co-determines the system of social division of labour and the social status hierarchy. A vocational training system must
4. also act as a labour market regulator, i.e. be able to remove surplus workforce from the market; it must
5. exhibit an economic dimension in the sense that both the sponsors and the clientele of the system must be promised financial advantage from participation in or going through the system. Last but not least, a vocational training system must
6. integrate the new generations into the existing socio-economic system, i.e. equip them with appropriate patterns of thinking, behaviour and loyalty.

5.2 Making the system functions operational

If we wish to examine the efficiency of a national or regional vocational training sector it is necessary to allocate the relatively abstract functions as-

---

129 Cf. Franzke, R.: Berufsausbildung und Arbeitsmarkt. Funktionen und Probleme des "dualen" Systems, (= Studien und Berichte des Max-Planck-Institutes für Bildungsforschung, Bd. 39), Berlin 1978, p. 11 ff.

certained to *measuring operations*, which can be used to ensure that the relevant sub-functions can be examined as unambiguously as possible, and not on the basis of intuitive criteria.

However, we cannot take logically unambiguous deduction proceedings as a basis for this operationalisation process and must instead operate with plausibility criteria and take the consensus capacity of indicators as a measure of their validity[130].

To this extent the following examination indicators for the various sub-functions can only be an initial suggestion which is essentially dependent on a process of consensus formation.

5.2.1 The qualification function

Here it is a matter of providing data capable of showing the quantitative efficiency of the vocational training sector, and also, for the sake of orientation, of the general training system.

• Duration of compulsory general schooling; entry and leaving rates related to the level of qualification of the general school system (primary stage, secondary stage, university).
• Transition rates into vocational training courses (colleges/university, polytechnic schools, vocational training centres, apprenticeships, short courses, etc.)
• Coverage rate of the measures towards initial vocational training in relation to the cohorts of the 15 to 19 year old youth (in school, out of school)
• Participation of the working population (19 to 64 years) in general and vocational further training measures
• Level of qualification of the working population according to level of training (university, technical college, apprenticeship/skilled worker training, unqualified)
• Global data on labour shortages/surpluses in the formal and informal private sector.

---

130 Cf. Meyer, H. L.: Trainingsprogramm zur Lernzielanalyse, 3rd edn., Frankfurt a.M. 1975, p. 67 ff.

5.2.2 The allocation function

Here it is a matter of providing data which sheds light on the qualitative efficiency of the vocational training sector with regard to the equal provision of as many economic areas as possible with qualified labour at the various qualification levels.

- Distribution of trainees to the various economic sectors or vocational fields (initial training)
- Annual examinations at the various vocational qualification levels (skilled labour, master craftsmen/technicians, university graduates)
- Data on the relationship between the employment structure and qualification structure of the training sector (initial training)
- Transition to employment; average waiting times for a job; usefulness (= relevance to practice) of the qualifications obtained
- Extent of vocational switching; usefulness of the preliminary qualifications obtained; problems of familiarization with the job
- Structural discrepancies between the training and employment of skilled workers.

5.2.3 The selection and status distribution function

Here it would be a matter of shedding light on the relationship between the vocational training sector and social mobility, or more precisely: does the system of vocational qualification help to cement social inequality or do its structural determinants tend to dissolve or neutralise this?

- Access to the vocational training sector according to the criteria: general education certificate and social status
- Internal differentiation mechanisms of the vocational training systems with regard to vocational status and social status
- Discrimination effects of the vocational training sector compared with specific social groups and minorities
- Comparison of employment structure and typical acquisition of qualifications (self-employed, family members assisting with the business, civil servants, blue-collar workers)
- Relationship between the pay structure and the qualifications obtained by employed persons

- Extent of vocational mobility and upward vocational mobility.

5.2.4 The absorption and preservation function

Here it is a matter of providing data which sheds light on the flexibility of the training sector against the background of varying economic conditions and demographic trends. Moreover, we need to examine whether and in what way measures outside the system are used to increase training capacities in times of a shortage of training places.

- Average proportion of total unemployment accounted for by youth unemployment (16 to 25 years) (time series)
- Youth unemployment in comparison with countries with differing training systems (e.g. EU or OECD countries)
- Supply situation in the vocational training sector in times of economic growth and normal demand for training places (time series)
- Supply situation in the vocational training sector in times of economic downturn and increased demand for training places (time series)
- Extent of the use of qualification measures outside the system, e.g. in times of a shortage of training places
- Transition of those completing training measures outside the system into training relationships or into the employment system.

5.2.5 The utilization function

Here it would be a matter of shedding light on the training motives of the private and state sponsors of vocational training which relate to the immediate economic advantages of becoming involved in training. Also of interest is whether the trainees or their parental homes gain immediate economic advantage from vocational training. Last but not least, we must identify the economic effects of vocational training hoped for in the long term and mention actual programmes in relation to this.

- Immediate financial motive for the involvement of (*private*) *companies* in vocational training
- Immediate financial motive for the involvement of *other private sponsors* in vocational training
- Financial motive of the trainees or their families for a training place

- Vocational training as a factor of production; the position of vocational training in political programmes and economic theories
- Vocational training as an instrument of economic promotion; actual concepts and projects
- Vocational training as an advantage of a particular location in international economic competition; estimates by politicians, economists and scientists.

5.2.6 The integration function

Here it is a matter of examining whether the institutions of a vocational training sector exercise educational functions or merely impart technical qualifications (skills and knowledge). Also of interest is the extent to which attempts are made to integrate minorities and/or disadvantaged social groups socially via vocational training. Objective data on the actual integration effect is naturally difficult to obtain.

- Training versus education; does the vocational training system – at least in concept – perform educational functions?
- Programmes for the disadvantaged within the context of the vocational training sector (school drop-outs, special students, foreigners, etc.)
- Programmes for the integration of disabled persons within the context of the vocational training sector
- Programmes for the vocational rehabilitation of adults
- Data on the relationship between (youth) criminality, (youth) employment and the lack of training opportunities
- Vocational training as a precondition for the formation of ''social identity''.

5.3 Functional analysis of the dual system of vocational training in the Federal Republic of Germany

The following functional analysis of the dual system in the Federal Republic of Germany is based primarily on the vocational training report which is published annually, the "Basic and structural data" published by the former Federal Ministry of Education and Science, again annually, and numerous relevant special surveys, above all by the Institute for Labour Market and Vocational Research in Nuremburg and the Federal Institute for Vocational Training in Berlin.

5.3.1 The qualification function of the dual system of vocational training

Experience may prove that vocational training cannot develop into an effective tool unless supported by an efficient general school system[131].

5.3.1.1   In Germany compulsory general schooling (currently 9-10 years, depending on the Federal state) has been in force more or less consistently since the beginning of the century, and the three-year compulsory vocational schooling (part-time compulsory schooling) since around the 1930s. Thus overall there is a total of 12 years compulsory schooling in the Federal Republic. The proportion of young people leaving the school system without any qualifications in 1992 was 7.9 % (as a percentage of the population of the same age)[132]. Of these youths, some subsequently obtain a lower school leaving certificate at vocational school (**Table 9**).

---

131 Cf. Vocational and Technical Education and Training. A World Bank Policy Paper, Washington D.C. 1991
132 Regarding the following figures cf. Federal German Ministry of Education and Science (BMBW) (Publisher): Grund- und Strukturdaten 1993/94, Bonn 1993, p. 72 ff.

Table 9: School leavers according to type of leaving certificate as a percentage of the population of the same age

Year	Leavers completing compulsory schooling[1]				Leavers with intermediate school leaving certificate or equivalent[2]		
	Total	of which			Total	of which from	
		without lower school leaving cert.		with		general schools	vocational schools
		Total	of which from special schools	Total			
Former West Germany							
1960	70.6	17.2	2.7	53.4	15.1	13.2	1.9
1965	70.5	16.8	3.4	52.9	16.8	11.9	4.8
1970	60.3	17.3	4.1	43.0	24.9	17.9	7.0
1975	48.3	12.0	4.5	36.3	34.4	25.1	9.3
1980	46.8	10.2	3.5	36.6	39.2	30.4	8.8
1981	42.8	9.5	3.1	33.3	40.5	31.4	9.1
1982	44.2	9.3	3.0	34.9	41.2	32.8	8.3
1983	45.0	9.1	3.0	35.9	42.8	34.2	8.6
1984	45.2	8.8	2.8	36.4	44.0	36.0	8.0
1985	45.4	8.3	2.8	37.1	44.3	36.9	7.5
1986	44.0	8.2	2.7	35.8	45.5	37.9	7.5
1987	44.1	8.0	3.6	36.0	45.2	38.1	7.1
1988	43.3	8.4	3.8	34.9	45.0	37.8	7.3
1989	42.2	8.6	3.7	33.6	44.9	37.4	7.6
1990	40.6	8.6	3.6	32.0	44.0	36.3	7.7
1991	39.5	8.5	3.4	31.0	42.9	35.6	7.3
1992[4]	39.7	8.7	3.4	31.0	43.0	36.0	7.0
New Federal States							
1992[5]	13.2	5.1	1.7	8.1	49.4	49.1	0.2
Germany							
1992	33.9	7.9	3.0	26.1	44.3	38.7	5.6

1 As a percentage of the average year group of the 15 to 17 year population
2 As a percentage of the average year group of the 16 to 18 year population
3 As a percentage of the average year group of the 18 to 21 year population
4 Including East Berlin
5 Excluding East Berlin

Source: Basic and structural data 1993/94, pages 72f.

Also: **School leavers according to type of leaving certificate as a percentage of the population of the same age**

Leavers with university entrance qualification[3]									Year
Total			General			Technical			
total	of which from		total	of which from		total	of which from		
	gen. sch.	voc. sch.		gen. sch.	voca. sch.		gen. sch.	voc. sch.	
Former West Germany									
6.1	6.1	–	–	6.1	–	–	–	–	1960
7.5	7.5	–	–	7.5	–	–	–	–	1965
11.3	10.3	1.0	10.7	10.3	0.5	0.5	–	0.5	1970
20.2	13.8	6.4	14.6	13.3	1.2	5.6	0.5	5.1	1975
21.7	15.6	6.1	16.5	15.2	1.3	5.2	0.4	4.8	1980
24.6	17.8	6.8	18.8	17.3	1.5	5.8	0.5	5.4	1981
26.8	19.0	7.8	20.1	18.4	1.7	6.7	0.6	6.1	1982
28.4	19.9	8.5	21.2	19.3	1.9	7.2	0.6	6.6	1983
28.5	20.2	8.3	21.6	19.7	1.9	6.9	0.6	6.3	1984
28.5	20.6	7.9	22.0	20.0	2.0	6.5	0.6	5.9	1985
28.4	20.6	7.8	21.9	20.1	1.8	6.5	0.6	6.0	1986
29.6	21.2	8.4	22.5	20.6	1.9	7.1	0.5	6.5	1987
31.5	22.0	9.6	23.6	21.5	2.2	8.0	0.5	7.5	1988
32.0	21.8	10.2	23.5	21.2	2.3	8.5	0.6	7.9	1989
33.5	22.5	11.0	24.4	21.8	2.5	9.1	0.7	8.5	1990
37.3	24.8	12.5	26.9	24.0	2.9	10.4	0.7	9.6	1991
35.7	23.4	12.4	25.6	22.6	3.0	10.2	0.8	9.4	1992[4]
New Federal States									
19.8	14.4	5.4	17.6	14.3	3.3	2.2	0.1	2.1	1992[5]
Germany									
32.7	21.7	11.1	24.1	21.0	3.0	8.7	0.7	8.0	1992

1 As a percentage of the average year group of the 15 to 17 year population
2 As a percentage of the average year group of the 16 to 18 year population
3 As a percentage of the average year group of the 18 to 21 year population
4 Including East Berlin
5 Excluding East Berlin

Source: Basic and structural data 1993/94, pages 72f.

In relation to cohorts of 15 to 17 year olds and of 16 to 18 year olds, in 1992

- 26.1 % obtained a lower school leaving certificate
- 44.3 % obtained an intermediate school leaving certificate

In relation to cohorts of 18 to 21 year olds and of 16 to 18 year olds

- 32.7 % obtained a university entrance qualification.

5.3.1.2   Access to vocational training is possible from all these levels of education; in this respect there are no restrictions. The previous schooling of the trainees in the dual system is shown in **Table 10**. It shows that the previous education structure of the trainees in the old Federal states has barely changed in recent years, since the structure of school leavers has stabilised. The proportion of lower school students with a certificate has varied around the 35 % mark, whilst that of intermediate school students has remained around a third. Entrance from the basic vocational training year has also become less significant, whilst the entrance of trainees with university entrance qualifications continues to increase (14.6 %). In the training area of trade and industry every fifth trainee already has an entrance qualification for university or technical college.

5.3.1.3   In statistical terms the dual system, which dominates absolutely in vocational training, captures around 75 % of 16 to 19 year olds (1990). Due to the shift in the age structure (average age in 1990: 18.7 years) reference to 16 to 19 year olds is becoming increasingly obsolete in statements on the participation of a year group in training. The age distribution of the trainees is very much broader. If we relate new entries of each age group to the dual system to the relevant population of the same age group and add the individual access rates (15-30 year olds) it emerges that in 1990 just over 66.5 % of this age group took up a company apprenticeship and 27 % a university or technical college course[133]. The proportion of youth taking up vocational training in the vocational trade school can be disregarded since the majority go into the dual system after obtaining basic vocational training.

---

133 Cf. Tessaring, M.: Das duale System der Berufsausbildung in Deutschland: Attraktivität und Beschäftigungsperspektiven, in: Mitteilungen aus der Arbeitsmarkt- und Berufsforschung 26 (1993), 131-161, p. 135 f.

Table 10: **Previous schooling of trainees according to training areas in the old Federal states in 1991 and 1992 and in the new Federal states in 1992 in percent**

Training area[1]	Trainees with previous schooling[2]													
	Lower school				Realschule (intermedia-teschool) or equivalent		University or tech. college entrance qualification		In-school basic vocational training year		Vocational trade school		Vocational preparatory year	
	without certificate		with certificate											
	1991	1992	1991	1992	1991	1992	1991	1992	1991	1992	1991	1992	1991	1992
Trade and industry	0.6	0.6	29.1	29.6	33.9	33.7	20.0	20.3	2.9	2.7	13.0	12.6	0.5	0.6
Manual trades[3]	6.2	6.4	53.6	53.7	20.6	20.4	6.0	6.1	6.1	6.1	6.0	5.8	1.4	1.6
Agriculture	4.8	5.2	25.9	26.8	27.5	27.8	14.7	16.1	23.0	20.4	3.6	3.1	0.5	0.6
Civil service	0.1	0.1	13.6	12.8	56.3	55.7	18.0	18.0	6.9	7.9	5.1	5.5	0.1	0.1
Freelance professions	0.6	0.7	22.8	27.5	53.4	50.6	13.8	12.8	0.7	0.7	7.2	7.2	0.2	0.5
Domestic science[4]	30.8	34.0	32.3	31.8	6.3	6.1	0.6	0.5	9.5	8.2	15.0	14.5	5.5	4.9
Ocean navigation[3]	1.0	–	33.8	16.5	33.0	30.7	30.7	50.5	1.4	2.2	–	–	–	–
All areas	**2.6**	**2.8**	**35.8**	**36.6**	**32.2**	**31.8**	**14.6**	**14.5**	**4.3**	**4.2**	**9.7**	**9.3**	**0.8**	**0.9**
New states/ East Berlin	–	**4.1**	–	**23,2**	–	**65.8**	–	**4.2**	–	**0.4**	–	**1.4**	–	**0.9**

Cf. Vocational training report 1993, summary 40, page 57.
1 Data per area for old Federal states only
2 Each trainee is listed only once, either according to the certificate obtained most recently or the school last attended. Percentages do not include the category "No data"; other schools divided between lower school with certificate and vocational trade school (T+I and M).
3 Calculated on the basis of data for recent successful leavers.
4 Domestic science in the municipal sector.

Source: Federal Statistics Office, series 11, Education and Culture, series 3, Vocational Training, surveyed as at 31 December; calculations by the Federal Institute for Vocational Training.

Source: Vocational Training Report 1994, page 60.

5.3.1.4   In 1991 37 % of all Germans in the age group from 19 to 64 years participated in further training measures. The participation rate in *vocational further training* is 21 %. However, the high overall rate of participation in further training takes on a rather different look when we look at individual groups[134]. It is still true that persons already having a good qualification more often try or more often have the opportunity to improve themselves further than those less qualified. Thus employed persons with a university entrance qualification are four or five times more likely to participate in further vocational training activities than the unskilled (**Table 11**). Vocational further training is particularly significant for *women* in order to increase their opportunities on the labour market.

5.3.1.5   The level of training of those in employment in all the Federal states is shown in **Table 12**. According to this, 72 % of all those in employment have completed an apprenticeship (= training in the dual system), 4 % have graduated from a technical college and 8 % from a scientific university. 16 % had no vocational training. Whilst the proportion of adults without training in the 40 to 50 year old age group is still just over 27 %, in the 20 to 30 age group (the baby boom years) it has fallen to 13 %; 90 % of the "new blood" starting their careers have a qualification from vocational training or university[135].

5.3.1.6   Older investigations regarding shortages of skilled labour conclude that the structural problems of the shortage of skilled labour have nothing to do with a quantitative undersupply in this market[136]. In contrast to what is frequently assumed, in global terms the number of trained skilled workers is far in excess of the demand for skilled labour or the number of skilled places available. What is decisive for the difficulties which occur periodically is that skilled workers largely migrate to other areas of the economy and other vocational fields from which they cannot be enticed back in times of demand.

---

134 Ditto, p. 244; BMBW (Publisher): Berichtssystem Weiterbildung 1991, (=Schriftenreihe Studie zu Bildung und Wissenschaft, Volume 110), Bonn 1993
135 Cf. Berufsbildungsbericht 1990, p. 1
136 Cf. Friedrich, W./H. v. Henniges: Facharbeitermangel: Umfang und strukturelle Hintergründe, in: Mitteilungen aus der Arbeitsmarkt- und Berufsforschung 15 (1982), 9-19

Table 11: German participants in vocational further training amongst 19-64 year olds[1] according to personal characteristics from 1979 to 1991 in percent

Characteristic	Participation rate				1991		
	1979	1982	1985	1988	all Germany	old Federal states	new Federal states
Total	10	12	12	18	21	25	20
Capacity for work							
Employed	15	17	17	25	27	26	29
Not employed	1	2	2	6	8	7	15
Employment by sex							
Men	17	20	18	27	29	29	30
Women	12	14	15	21	24	23	28
Employment according to qualification groups							
No vocational training	8	3	3	9	–	11	8[3]
Apprentice/voc. trade school	14	14	15	21	–	22	23
Master's school/other trade school	23	22	26	37	–	38	40[4]
University	24	33	31	41	–	43	48
Employment acc. to vocational position							
Blue-collar workers	8	8	5	12	16	15	17
White-collar workers	18	19	21	29	33	32	40
Officers	27	32	28	40	37	37	–[5]
Self-employed	12	20	16	25	26	25	37
Employment acc. to size of company							
1 to 99 employees	11	13	13	17	22	20	28
100 to 999 employees	12	10	14	20	23	22	25
1000+ employees	17	19	22	31	32	33	29

1 Representative survey of around 800 people (1979), 3500 people (1982, 1985) and 7000 people (1988 and 1991). From 1991 expanded Federal territory.
2 Not shown since the training courses in the old and new Federal states are not comparable.
3 Including semi-skilled workers
4 Trade school training in the new Federal states is not directly comparable with that in the old Federal states.
5 Figures inadequate.

Source: Federal Minister for Education and Science, Education and Science News 12/92 and additional evaluations.

Source: Vocational Training Report 1993, page 138

Table 12: Highest training qualification according to sex in percent

Qualification/sex	Germans in employment in the old Federal states 1979	Germans in employment in the old Federal states 1985/86	Germans in employment in the old Federal states 1991/92	Foreigners surveyed in the old Federal states 1991/92	In employment in the new Federal states 1991/92	In total in employment in the Federal Republic of Germany 1991/92
Total in employment						
Without qualification	30	24	16	51	5	16
Apprenticeship only	50	56	56	36	57	55
Trade school[1]	12	9	16	5	25	17
Technical college	3	3	4	1	3	4
University	6	7	8	7	10	8
Total	**100**	**100**	**100**	**100**	**100**	**100**
Absolute surveyed	**27709**	**26515**	**23476**	**614**	**7851**	**31941**
Men						
Without qualification	22	17	11	45	3	12
Apprenticeship only	54	50	55	40	57	54
Trade school	15	12	20	6	25	20
Technical college	3	4	5	1	3	4
University	6	7	9	7	12	10
Total	100	100	100	100	100	100
Absolute surveyed	17653	16519	14656	467	4054	19177
Women						
Without qualification	44	35	23	62	7	21
Apprenticeship only	43	53	59	29	56	57
Trade school	8	4	10	3	26	13
Technical college	1	2	2	0	2	2
University	4	7	7	6	9	7
Total	100	100	100	100	100	100
Absolute surveyed	10056	9996	8820	147	3797	12764

1 This data has been tailored to structures of the relevant microcensus surveys. To do multidimensional weighting programmes were set for each surveying institution. Departures for the trade schools in the 1985/86 survey are primarily due to such weighting procedures.

Source: BiBB/IAB surveys 1979, 1985/86, 1991/92

Source: Vocational Training Report 1993, page 129

According to an investigation by BiBB/IAB[137] only 58 % of people trained as skilled workers could be kept in the vocation learned; 42 % migrated, most of them immediately after training.

5.3.2 The allocation function of the dual system

Vocational training systems capable of supplying specifically qualified workers to almost all areas of the economy and almost all vocational fields are the exception rather than the rule. By far the majority of the existing training systems exclusively serve the modern areas of the economy (trade, industry, modern services) and neglect the traditional or informal economic sector.

5.3.2.1 **Tables 13 and 14** show the number of trainees in the various chamber areas representing the different economic sectors. It is clear just from this list that vocational training is carried out according to the norms of the dual system in practically all the economic sectors in Germany. Although the degree of involvement varies depending on the company size category[138] and economic group (or vocational group), the inclusion of the entire spectrum of vocations in the training system is not in question. This is evidenced by the range of state recognised training vocations[139]. Vocational groups not encompassed, or hardly encompassed by the dual system such as the health and teaching vocations are trained in what are known as ''vocational training centres'' (= full-time training; 1992: 253,200 students).

5.3.2.2 The annual examinations at the various vocational qualification levels encompass the following numbers:

1. **University level**
 – graduates (1991) 196,320

2. **Intermediate qualification level**
 – master craftsman's exams (M) 45,630

---

137 BiBB/IAB: Qualifikation und Berufsverlauf, Berlin 1981
138 Cf. Greinert, Das ''deutsche System'' ..., loc. cit., p. 118 f.
139 Cf. Benner, H.: Der Ausbildungsberuf als berufspädagogisches und bildungsökonomisches Problem, Hanover 1977

Table 13: Trainees according to training area in the old Federal states, 1975 to 1991

Year	Trainees Total	of which in training area						
		trade & industry[1]	manual trades	agricul-ture	civil service	freelance professions	domestic science[2]	ocean naviga-tion
1975	1328925	633958	504662	32954	103172	45952	7319	908
1977	1397354	643817	556088	41003	103431	44841	7215	959
1979	1644619	748400	676215	46565	110422	53838	8136	1043
1981	1676877	771347	673564	46525	123646	54278	6624	893
1983	1722416	791895	674903	52003	130269	63723	8755	868
1985	1831501	874614	687454	53396	131458	72856	10641	1082
1987	1738687	865963	617823	44553	123055	71675	12799	819
1988	1657960	827213	577873	38515	133570	67310	12855	624
1989	1552534	783274	532546	33810	129253	62213	10955	483
1990	1476880	756416	486911	29748	130262	63445	9673	425
1991	1430211	734336	460417	27426	137393	61832	8320	487

1 Including banking, insurance, hotel and tourism
2 Domestic science in the municipal sector

Source: Federal Statistics Office, series 11, Education and Culture, series 3, Vocational Training 1991, surveyed as at 31 December

Source: Vocational Training Report 1993, page 53.

- intermediate skilled staff (T + I)
  - technical/industrial 20,190
  - commercial/administrative 35,430
- technical colleges 11,480

3. Skilled workers
- dual system (1992) 575,300
- vocational trade schools 49,180
(M = manual trades; T + I = trade & industry)

Table 14: Trainees according to training areas in the old and new Federal states in percent

	Old Federal states	New Federal states
Trade & industry	49.7	54.3
of which:		
Industrial vocations	19.3	30.9
Commercial and technical vocations	30.4	23.4
Manual trades	33.1	33.7
Agriculture	1.8	3.0
Civil service	4.5	3.3
Freelance professions	10.3	4.1
Domestic science	0.5	1.5
Ocean navigation	0.1	0.1

Source: Federal Statistics Office, series 11, Education and Culture, series 3, Vocational Training 1992, surveyed as at 31 December; calculations by the Federal Institute for Vocational Training

Source: Vocational Training Report 1994, page 55

This list gives only a cursory impression since numerous so-called ''further training examinations'' are not included (e.g. manual trades 1991: 15,678 participants). Some graduates of technical colleges are included in the master craftsman's examinations and vocational trade school examinations in the final examinations in the dual system. However, what should be clear is the relative restriction of opportunities for formal qualifications at the various levels of qualification.

5.3.2.3   The extent to which a vocational training system is tailored to the qualification needs of the employment system in quantitative and qualitative terms can be checked empirically. **Table 15** provides a comparison of the vocational structure of the trainees and of employed persons over a period of ten years. What is particularly conspicuous is that the employment trend and the qualification trend in the areas of ''manufacturing/maintenance'' and ''services/infrastructure tasks'' are moving in opposite directions. Contrary to the general trend towards service vocations found generally in industrial countries, and to which the Federal Republic of Germany also adheres, vocational training in the manufacturing vocations has increased in the period specified whilst training for service vocations has decreased. Major discrepancies between the proportion of the employed and the qualification volume are recognisable, particularly in the vocational groups ''installation and maintenance of technical plant'', ''planning and laboratory vocations'', ''commercial service staff'', ''services related to objects'' and ''infrastructure tasks''.

Although this shortcoming is neutralised somewhat by vocational switching, further training and full-time school education, the German training system has undoubtedly not yet adjusted sufficiently to the economic restructuring and ''mismanagement tendencies'' can be found[140].

5.3.2.4   Considerable imbalance between employment and training was found as long ago as 1970 in a survey of careers carried out by the Institute for Labour Market and Vocational Research (IAB). According to this study, in 1970 61 % of all trained workers had been trained in a manual trade, but 47 % were employed in industry, 28 % in other areas of the economy and only 25 % in manual trades. "Of the total of 3.9 million male workers trained in manual trades only 1.4 million were still employed in the manual trades and 2.5 million had switched to other economic sectors (1.5 million in industry and 1.0 million in other economic sectors)". The trend towards qualitative over-qualification in the manual trades has since been confirmed in all subsequent investigations of vocational and training courses[141].

---

140 Cf. Greinert, Das ''deutsche System'' ..., loc. cit., p. 154 ff.
141 Cf. Hofbauer, H.: Strukturdiskrepanzen zwischen Bildungs- und Beschäftigungssystem im Bereich der betrieblichen Berufsausbildung für Facharbeiterberufe, in: Mitteilungen aus der Arbeitsmarkt- und Berufsforschung 10 (1977), 252-257; Stegmann, H./H. Kraft: Ausbildungs- und Berufswege von 23-24jährigen, in: Mitteilungen aus der Arbeitskraft- und Berufsforschung 20 (1987), 142-163

Table 15: Comparison of the vocational structure of trainees and persons in employment in 1977, 1980 and 1986 (in percent[1])

Vocational groups		1977	1980	1986
		%	%	%
1. Manufacturing and maintenance	A	45.25	47.59	47.16
	B	38.57	37.70	36.22
1.1 Extraction of natural products	A	2.78	3.38	3.52
	B	1.37	1.37	1.56
1.2 Extraction of mineral resources	A	0.11	0.35	0.60
	B	0.78	0.65	0.61
1.3 Production of stone, prod., goods	A	1.93	1.94	2.06
	B	8.06	7.63	6.97
1.4 Manufacture of consumer goods	A	6.01	7.20	7.17
	B	7.80	7.46	7.01
1.5 Construction, development	A	6.77	9.61	9.64
	B	7.93	8.03	7.15
1.5.1 Construction	A	2.25	4.04	3.79
	B	4.71	4.77	3.05
1.5.2 Development	A	4.52	5.57	5.58
	B	3.21	3.26	3.20
1.6 Installation and maintenance of technical plant	A	27.66	25.12	24.17
	B	12.63	12.56	12.92
2. Services, infra-structure tasks	A	54.75	52.41	52.84
	B	61.43	62.30	63.78
2.1 Services	A	54.66	52.25	52.25
	B	52.98	54.15	56.78

Vocational groups		1977	1980	1986
		%	%	%
2.1.1 Planning and laboratory vocations	A	3.34	2.62	2.63
	B	6.13	6.25	6.71
2.1.2 Administrative and office vocations	A	15.50	14.71	16.30
	B	17.80	18.02	18.41
2.1.3 Commercial service staff	A	22.05	21.43	20.06
	B	10.80	11.05	11.58
2.1.4 Services related to people	A	9.41	8.85	8.28
	B	7.35	8.13	9.72
2.1.5 Services related to objects	A	4.35	4.63	5.25
	B	10.91	10.69	10.36
2.2 Infrastructure tasks	A	0.09	0.16	0.33
	B	8.45	8.15	6.99
Total	A	100.00	100.00	100.00
	B	100.00	100.00	100.00

1. A. Percentages for trainees calculated according to the proportions of successful examination candidates (without multiple counting due to stage training)
    B. Percentages of persons in employment paying social security contributions.

Source: Vocational Training Report 1989, page 66.

One of the consequences of this is that when moving to working life after completing training, over half of those trained in companies leave the company in which they were trained within two years of completing their training.

The size of company is the most significant indicator here. The proportion of those leaving the training company after completing training increases from 17 % in training companies with 1000 or more employees through 22 % in companies with 500 to 1000 employees to 34 % in training companies with 5 to 9 employees and 42 % in those with less than 5 people[142].

Despite all this, association with the company is commonly believed to be an advantage of training in the dual system compared with in-school vocational training courses. If we include everyone who has been trained in the dual system in the observation, in the old Federal states 79 % obtained an adequate job immediately after training, 8 % initially had to make do with another job and 3 % took further training. Only 2 % had to accept a temporary period of unemployment[143]. These rates are unlikely to be reached with any school-oriented training system.

The Federal German Institute for Vocational Training (BiBB) and the Institute for Labour Market and Vocational Research (IAB) carry out six-yearly surveys of training and the transition to employment. The latest was carried out in 1991/92. Regarding the usefulness (= relevance to practice) of the apprenticeship, those who had completed the apprenticeship were asked how much of their vocational knowledge and skills acquired during the apprenticeship they were still able to use in their everyday working life.

Usefulness of apprenticeship

Very little/nothing	15
Little	9
Some	17
Quite a lot	21
A great deal	35

Source: BiBB/IAB survey 1991/92

Remaining in the economic sector in which training was given was of crucial importance for the usefulness of the training. Whilst the proportions of those still employed in their training area claiming little or no usefulness are below 20 %, amongst those who have switched to another economic sector this indicator rises to values above 40 %[144].

---

142 Berufsbildungsbericht 1993, S. 131
143 Ditto, p. 131 f; however, the IAB survey of experts produces less positive figures: between 1989 and 1991 only 55 % of leavers obtained permanent employment and a further 11 % temporary employment. 15 % left the labour market to complete national service; cf. Chaberny, A. et al: Beschäftigungsaussichten und berufliche Anforderungen in anerkannten Ausbildungsberufen – Ergebnisse einer Befragung betrieblicher Experten (= Beiträge zur Arbeitsmarkt- und Berufsforschung, Nr. 146), Nuremberg 1991

5.3.2.5   The BiBB has carried out some long-term studies into remaining in vocations and changes of vocation[145]. In that carried out most recently the careers of those trained in metalworking, electrical engineering and commerce/administration were investigated.

Immediately after their final exams approx. 70 % of the young skilled workers were employed in their trained vocation. Six months later this figure had already fallen to 56 %, which may well be due to the termination of contracts of employment prior to expiry of the trial period. However, at this point those who have completed their national service or have completed a so-called "family phase" begin to return to their trained vocation. There is also a return to the trained vocation through switching companies (return rate: 25 %). After five years approx. 55 % of the workers surveyed are working in their trained vocation, 20 % have switched to another vocation and the rest are in further training (school or studying) or moving into "other activities" (unemployed, helping with the family, temporary workers). It is difficult to compare the switching rates determined with those of older cross-section surveys, according to which 40 % of those trained in companies switch trained vocation in the course of their careers[146].

The question of whether they are still able to utilize the skills and knowledge learned in their new area of activity tended to be answered in the negative by those who had changed vocation. Despite this, in the past around three quarters of all vocational changes were completed without formal training in the new vocation[147]. Vocational mobility against the background of dual vocational training tends to cause emotional problems rather than problems relating to qualifications.

5.3.2.6   These relatively extensive – if probably undramatic – vocational changes make it likely that there are considerable structural discrepancies between the training and employment of skilled workers.

---

144 Ditto, p. 132 f.
145 Cf. Westhoff, G./K. Schöngen: Der Prozeß beruflicher Integration junger Fachkräfte – eine Längsschnittanalyse, Berlin/Bonn 1993; Zusammenfassung in: Berufsbildungsbericht 1993, p. 134 f.
146 Cf. e.g. BiBB/IAB: Qualifikation und Berufsverlauf, Berlin 1981
147 Cf. Franzke, Berufsausbildung und Arbeitsmarkt ..., loc. cit. p. 45 ff.

This is in fact the case: in 1989 a total of 15 % of all male and 18 % of all female trained workers were classified as non-skilled workers. There has been a noticeable increase in the tendency to employ young trained staff in assisting and auxiliary positions between 1985 and 1989[148].

In some vocations the practice of status-inadequate employment is extremely marked. In particular these include the male-dominated vocational areas of metalworker, mechanic and fitter (increase in status-inadequate employment between 1980 and 1989: 63 %), electrician (increase: 57 %) and technical vocations (increase: approx. 30 %). In the other metal-related vocations the use of male staff for non-skilled activities increased to over 50 %.

There are also such extreme discrepancies with regard to the use of young skilled workers (up to 26 years) in the various economic sectors: in the production of man-made fibres 41 % of young skilled workers, in the manufacture of motor vehicles 40%, in tobacco processing 32 %, in iron and steel production 31 %, in the manufacturing and processing of glass 30 % and in rubber and asbestos processing 28 % are employed below the level of skilled worker. The proportion of women in employment inadequate for their status is even higher in some sectors in which large companies generally dominate, which guarantee a good income and have a good position in the employment market.

---

148 Cf. Henniges, H. v.: Ausbildung und Verbleib von Facharbeitern. Eine empirische Analyse für die Zeit von 1980 bis 1989, (= Beiträge zur Arbeitsmarkt- und Berufsforschung, Nr. 155), Nuremberg 1991

5.3.3 The selection and status distribution function of the dual system of vocational training

According to the unanimous result of vocational sociological research[149], vocation and vocational training tend to reinforce social structures and thus make a significant contribution to the maintenance of social inequality. Upward social mobility is the exception rather than the rule and restricted to a few "climbing channels", even in open, democratically organised societies.

5.3.3.1   The dual system of vocational training in Germany was originally designed for members of the lower middle classes as a "continuing" training institution and for a long time was kept strictly separate in legal, institutional and ideological terms from the general school system, and particularly from academic training courses. It was characterised by a specific standard biography of traditional three-level schooling: from leavers of the Volksschule (later Hauptschule) (lower school), whose social origin marked the upper or lower bottom level.

This has changed fundamentally. Whilst in 1970 around 80 % of trainees still came from the lower school, 10 years later these amounted to only 50 %; in 1990 the percentage had fallen still further (35.5 %). In return, the percentage of those leaving the intermediate school (Realschule) had increased to 31.8 % and those with the German equivalent of ''A'' levels to 14.2 %. In 1991 30 % of those commencing study at universities had completed training in the dual system. The dual system has evidently lost its function of clear and open status distribution.

5.3.3.2   Nevertheless, differentiation into strata correlating largely to training certificates still takes place within the dual system, oriented towards the attractiveness of the training vocations. Thus the equivalent of ''A'' level students tend to take up the commercial training vocations which are in great demand: around 60 % of trainees in the vocations of bank clerk and insurance clerk are ''A'' level students and the proportion amongst commercial trainees in industry, shipping and social security is around 40 %.

---

149 Cf. Beck, U./M. Brater/H. Daheim: Soziologie der Arbeit und der Berufe, Reinbek 1980, p. 42 ff.

If the commercial and service training vocations dominate in the scale of popularity amongst those with an intermediate school leaving certificate, lower school leavers tend to choose manufacturing vocations in industry and manual trades. School drop-outs and special students have to be content with unattractive manual trade and service vocations (see **Tables 16 – 19**). These clear preferences show that the dual system has not yet adjusted to the changed clientele. In the manufacturing sector in particular, vocational careers capable of competing with those in the services sector in terms of demand and payment must be offered.

5.3.3.3   In its classical form the dual system was a training facility for the "gifted sons of the people" (Lutz); it offered the elite of Volksschule leavers a chance to acquire skilled status. This system of qualification largely excluded those less successful at school just as much as those leaving with higher school leaving certificates. Even in the early seventies only 50 % of an age group completed vocational training organised along dual lines (1990: 75 %).

As shown above, this is very different today, and not least because of this, peripheral groups (e.g. the children of immigrants, special students, youths with criminal records, those with behavioural problems) still find it very difficult to obtain a successful qualification within the context of the dual training or even to obtain a training place. The reasons for this are to be found not only amongst the social deficits and social impairments of the youth concerned but are also due to the fact that the selection and recruitment of (private) companies has not been restricted in any way in respect of social policy requirements. In Germany there has been an awareness of the need for state intervention here for some years. Attempts are being made to improve the training opportunities of the peripheral youth via special "programmes for the disadvantaged" (see 6.2 and 6.3).

5.3.3.4   According to the last microcensus the employment structure in the old Federal states was as follows:
- self-employed   2,580,000
- helping with family business   578,000
- white-collar workers   15,201,000
- blue-collar workers   10,975,000

Table 16: **Trainees with university entrance qualifications in order of the ten most popular training vocations in 1992 in the old Federal states in 1991 and 1992[1]**

Training vocation	Trainees with university entrance qualifications		Proportion of trainees in the vocation in question	
	1991	1992	1991	1992
	Number		Percentage	
Bank clerk	33200	32600	58.2	56.1
Commercial asst. in industry	25500	23800	40.7	39.9
Comm. asst. in whole-sale & export trade	13200	12400	26.8	25.8
Asst. to tax & financial consultants	9100	9500	36.6	37.7
Insurance clerk	8500	8400	58.2	55.7
Office clerk (trade & industry only)	7100	5800	14.8	13.4
Hotel assistant	5300	5000	24.4	23.0
Social security clerk	4500	4800	39.2	37.7
Draughtsman	3600	4500	32.9	36.4
Shipping clerk	4900	4400	38.0	35.1

Cf. Vocational Training Report 1993. Summary 41. page 57.

1 Extrapolated values not including the category "no data"; in the case of manual trades and ocean navigation extrapolation based on data of newly qualified persons.

Source: Federal Statistics Office, series 11, Education and Culture, series 3, Vocational Training, surveyed as at 31 December; calculations by the Federal Institute for Vocational Training

Blue-collar workers principally obtain their vocational qualification in the dual system, followed by white-collar workers, those helping with a family business and sometimes (e.g. often in the manual trades) the self-employed. A master craftsman qualification is required in order to run a manual trade business, and training in the dual system is the basis of this. 30 % of those starting university in 1991 had completed training in the dual system. The majority of those attending technical college in particular had completed vocational training. Thus the dual vocational training system forms a wide-

Table 17:   Trainees with intermediate school leaving certificate or equivalent in order of the ten most popular training vocations in 1992 in the old Federal states in 1991 and 1992[1]

Training vocation	Trainees with inter-mediate school certi-ficate or equivalent		Proportion of trainees in the vocation in question	
	1991	1992	1991	1992
	Number		Percentage	
Medical assistant	25300	24100	54.9	50.6
Dental assistant	18100	18200	56.3	52.4
Commercial asst. in industry	18500	18100	29.5	30.3
Bank clerk	16300	17600	28.6	30.3
Retail assistant	19300	17300	29.4	28.2
Office clerk (trade & industry only)	18100	16400	37.7	38.2
Comm. asst. in whole-sale and export trade	16800	16400	34.2	34.1
Legal assistant	15500	15600	65.8	65.2
Car mechanic	12200	13800	19.0	18.4
Electrician	11300	10700	25.9	25.2

Cf. Vocational Training Report 1993. Summary 42. page 58.

1 Extrapolated values not including the category "no data".

Source: Federal Statistics Office, series 11, Education and Culture, series 3, Vocational Training, surveyed as at 31 December; calculations by the Federal Institute for Vocational Training

Source: Vocational Training Report 1994, page 61.

spread basis of qualification and experience for management in the private sector.

5.3.3.5   The *vocation of skilled labour* (skilled workman, journeyman, clerk, etc.) is a crucial feature of the recruitment and employment policy of companies and businesses in Germany. The vocation of skilled worker is a specific exchange of labour for income or remuneration. The companies

Table 18: Trainees with lower school leaving certificate in order of the ten most popular training vocations in 1992 in the old Federal states in 1991 and 1992[1]

Training vocation	Trainees with lower school leaving certificate		Proportion of trainees in the vocation in question	
	1991	1992	1991	1992
	Number		Percentage	
Car mechanic	39100	45900	60.8	61.4
Retail clerk	29600	29200	45.1	47.8
Hairdresser	29500	29500	67.5	67.6
Electrician	25000	26500	57.4	58.5
Medical assistant	13900	17400	30.2	36.5
Dental assistant	11900	14600	37.2	42.0
Plumber	14500	14500	64.6	65.8
Painter	14300	13400	61.0	59.7
Industrial mechanic – plant engineering	14500	13400	50.9	51.6
Industrial mechanic – mechanical and systems engineering	13900	13200	45.5	46.5

Cf. Vocational Training Report 1993. Summary 43. page 58.

1 Extrapolated values not including the category "no data"; in the case of manual trades based on data of newly qualified persons.

Source: Federal Statistics Office, series 11, Education and Culture, series 3, Vocational Training, surveyed as at 31 December; calculations by the Federal Institute for Vocational Training

link both particular expectations in respect of the capacity for work of the labour sought and ideas concerning the wage or salary costs incurred to the various vocational certificates. Vice versa, the persons practising the vocation associate expectations of income, working conditions and career opportunities with their certificates[150].

150 Ditto, p. 71 ff

Table 19: Trainees without lower school leaving certificate in order of the ten most popular training vocations in 1992 in the old Federal states in 1991 and 1992[1]

Training vocation	Trainees without lower school leaving certificate		Proportion of trainees in the vocation in question	
	1991	1992	1991	1992
	Number		Percentage	
Car mechanic	2800	3700	4.4	5.0
Painter	3500	3600	15.0	16.2
Hairdresser	2900	3000	6.7	7.7
Metal construction worker	1900	1800	11.2	10.1
Technical housekeeping assistant [2]	1600	1700	62.0	64.5
Bricklayer	1500	1600	9.0	9.1
Baker	1500	1500	10.2	11.9
Plumber	1500	1400	6.5	6.5
Joiner	1400	1200	4.6	3.9
Electrician	1100	1100	2.5	2.5

Cf. Vocational Training Report 1993. Summary 44. page 59.

1 Extrapolated values not including the category "no data"; in the case of manual trades extrapolation based on data of newly qualified persons.
2 Training vocation acc. to 48 VTA; includes housekeeping assistant.

Source: Federal Statistics Office, series 11, Education and Culture, series 3, Vocational Training, surveyed as at 31 December; calculations by the Federal Institute for Vocational Training

Source: Vocational Training Report 1994, page 62.

In Germany the level of income paid to skilled labour is essentially determined – apart from age, vocational group and economic sector – by training qualifications, sex and position in the vocation/company. **Table 20** shows the income gaps of persons in employment according to qualification and sex. It is conspicuous that the gap between unskilled workers and those who have completed the dual system is relatively small (although it increased between 1976 and 1989). There is a significant jump in income

116

only at the next level of qualification: in 1989 master craftsman, technician and other trade school graduates obtained an income 47 % higher than the average. Technical college and university graduates are substantially higher still.

Although the average incomes vary considerably according to position in the vocation/company position, as a whole there is a significant correlation between income level and level of qualifications regardless of vocational/ company position and sex[151].

Table 20: Income gaps[1] between persons in employment[2] according to qualification and sex in 1976 and 1989

Qualification	1976		1989	
	Men	Women	Men	Women
No qualifications	94	94	87	88
Apprentice/voc. trade sch.	100	103	95	100
Vocational school	124	128	147	119
Technical college	169	137	161	137
University	199	173	183	175
Total	100	100	100	100
Total (in DM)	1528	1124	2285	1659

Source: Tessaring, loc. cit., page 145.

5.3.3.6 The *branch switching* of skilled labour after training in Germany is relatively stable. The results of the BiBB/IAB survey of 1991/92 show that a good fifth of the skilled labour trained in the economic sector of "manual trades" migrate into industry and 26 % into other economic sectors. Only just over half those trained remain in the manual trades. There are similarly low retention rates in agriculture.

Vice versa, outside recruitment of qualified staff is highest in trade and in the civil service (78 % each). The proportion of skilled labour taken over by industry from the manual trades is 37 %[152].

---

151 Cf. Tessaring, M.: Das duale System der Berufsausbildung in Deutschland: Attraktivität und Beschäftigungsperspektiven, in: Mitteilungen aus der Arbeitsmarkt- und Berufsforschung 26 (1993), 131-161, p. 145
152 Ditto, p. 151

Promotion in the vocations for which qualifications are obtained in the dual system is controlled primarily by vocational further qualification. This has expanded greatly in recent years, i.e. the participation of persons in employment in further training has risen continuously in the period from 1987 to 1992[153]. However, this expansion has passed certain groups of qualified persons by (e.g. blue-collar workers, simple white-collar workers) and those in employment who have completed an apprenticeship or vocational trade school training are underrepresented, unlike in previous years. In contrast, the participation of persons with higher school and/or vocational training in further training is way above average[154].

This would make us conclude that the classical paths of promotion starting from the dual system – master craftsman, technician, specialist training – have lost attractiveness in the course of the expansion of training. One of the reasons for this is that the mean employment level is now threatened from "above" and "below"; from above by so-called "side entrants", i.e. graduates of technical universities and vocational academies, and from below by highly-qualified specialist workers with additional internal company qualifications[155]. Without clearly defined paths for promotion and promotional positions which can be chosen or reached following vocational training with a dual orientation, the loss of attractiveness of the dual system will continue at a brisk pace.

5.3.4 The absorption and preservation function of the dual system of vocational training

The absorptive capacity of a training system is proved above all if excess labour is to be kept away from the labour market because of economic downturn. In market-oriented systems this often works only if non-system conforming strategies and means are (additionally) used, or more precisely: if the state intervenes in the market mechanism.

5.3.4.1   In economic and socio-political terms youth unemployment marks a massive waste of skills, human energy and motivation. It affects a

---

153 Tessaring, loc. cit., p. 152
154 Ditto, p. 153
155 Cf. Drexel, I.: Das Ende des Facharbeiteraufstiegs? Frankfurt a.M./New York 1993

group of people (aged between 15 and 25) which requires particular devotion in respect of finding its identity and social integration. Excluding these youths or young adults from the area of socially organised work or from access to it has serious consequences for those affected as well as for society.

Table 21 shows the trend in youth unemployment in West Germany from 1984 to 1993 in comparison with the trend in the general unemployment rate. The high rate amongst 20 to 25 year olds is conspicuous, both in comparison with the general rate of unemployment and in comparison with 15-20 year olds. In other words, this group marks the difficult transition from training system to the employment system.

5.3.4.2 Experience from the past two decades shows that the extent of youth unemployment is fundamentally co-determined by the *nature of the vocational training system*. An international comparison from the 1970s already shows that countries with "dual" structured training (Switzerland, Austria, Germany) reported the lowest proportion of youth unemployment under 20 in comparison with countries with other systems (USA, UK, France)[156].

Table 22 also provides evidence of this statement within the context of the EC (now EU) countries. With the exception of the small state of Luxembourg, all the EC countries consistently reported higher rates of youth unemployment than West Germany. The highest rates are found in countries with vocational training organised in schools (France, Italy, Greece, Spain).

5.3.4.3 – 5.3.4.4 The absorption function of the German dual training system can best be analyzed in the phase known as "training catastrophe" – a time of excess demand for training places caused by demographic circumstances. In such a period one particular strength of this training model comes to the fore, namely its instrumental usefulness in reducing youth unemployment.

---

156 Cf. Petzold, H.-J. (Publisher): Jugend ohne Berufsperspektive, Weinheim/Basel 1976, p. 141

Table 21: Unemployment rate and youth unemployment rate in West Germany, 1984-1993

Year	Gen. rate	under 20 years	20 – 25 years	under 25 years
		% of all unemployed	% of all unemployed	total
1984	9.1	7.3	18.1	25.5
1985	9.3	7.7	17.6	24.3
1986	9.0	7.8	17.0	23.3
1987	8.9	5.6	16.0	21.6
1988	8.7	4.7	15.3	20.0
1989	7.9	3.9	13.4	17.2
1990	7.8	3.5	12.3	15.8
1991	6.3	3.4	11.8	15.2
1992				

Source: Statistical Yearbook of the FRG 1985-1993

Table 22: Unemployment rates in EC countries 1983-1991

	1983			1985			1989			1991		
	M	F	Yth	M	F	Yth	M	F	Yth	M	F	Yth
Belgium	8.7	19.1	27.5	7.6	18.6	25.4	5.5	13.3	18.1	5.4	12.6	18.8
Denmark	8.1	10.4	16.8	5.6	9.1	10.5	6.9	8.6	10.8	7.9	9.5	11.1
West Germany	6.1	8.0	11.9	6.1	8.7	10.1	4.5	7.2	5.5	3.7	5.2	3.8
Greece	5.8	11.7	22.8	5.6	11.7	22.9	4.6	12.4	24.8	4.3 1	11.7[1]	23.2[1]
Spain	16.5	20.9	42.7	20.1	25.2	48.2	12.8	25.0	33.9	12.0	23.0	30.5
France	6.3	10.8	21.5	8.3	12.5	25.4	7.0	12.4	20.4	7.4	12.6	20.2
Ireland	14.6	16.6	22.3	17.5	19.8	26.1	15.4	16.4	21.8	15.4	17.5	24.4
Italy	5.7	14.3	29.7	6.4	15.8	31.9	7.0	16.7	31.1	7.0	16.1	28.7
Luxembourg	2.6	5.2	8.1	2.2	4.4	6.8	1.4	2.8	4.3	1.4	3.0	4.7
Netherlands	11.2	14.7	22.4	9.2	12.8	17.8	6.3	11.9	13.1	4.8	10.5	9.9
Portugal	5.3	11.8	18.6	6.7	11.7	20.1	3.5	7.1	11.6	2.6	5.4	8.2
UK	11.8	9.8	20.0	11.7	11.0	18.3	7.3	6.9	10.2	10.1	8.3	14.6
EC	8.7	11.8	22.8	9.4	12.9	23.1	7.0	11.7	17.5	7.3	11.2	17.2

Source: Eurostat

Table 23 outlines the supply situation in the training sector from 1976 to 1985. What is primarily visible is the enormous steep increase in demand

120

for training during this period, but also the relatively rapid increase in the training offered on the part of the companies. It we take into account the fact that the training market which exists in Germany is an "offer market", i.e. the companies are not obliged to provide vocational training and suffer no disadvantage from not doing so, such flexibility may be considered extraordinary.

Table 2 (see page 42) shows the number of training relationships which actually existed in the years 1960-1992 in the various training areas. The following can be read off from this time series:

1. The quantitative efficiency ("capture rate") of the dual system. Between 1975 and 1985 the number of training places actually in existence increased by around 500,000.

This increase took place largely for sociopolitical motives; since the global economic crisis took effect in 1994, expansion of vocational training could hardly be justified on the basis of economic necessity. Nevertheless, the companies' anticyclical training behaviour makes financial sense because it provides the required workforce/qualification capacity when the economy picks up again.

2. We can recognise an over-proportional increase in training relationships in the areas which often make large net gains from vocational training (e.g. manual trades, agriculture).

The so-called "sponge function" of these training areas must however be considered ambivalent: in a short-term socio-political perspective it is certainly positive since numerous youth are saved from the fate of unemployment, at least at the start of their adult life; from a training policy – and also long-term sociopolitical – perspective it tends to be negative, since this excess training as a rule concerns vocations which neither offer solid job opportunities in the medium term nor can offer long-term job opportunities. However, what the trainees are left with are the extra-functional qualifications, which is why they are generally preferred to persons with no vocational training by the personnel managers of companies when taking on staff for skilled and unskilled activities.

121

3. The expansion of the training volume through the entry of the baby boomers to the dual system did however accelerate a shift in training structures towards global trends in the employment sector.

The service vocations, e.g. in trade, the civil service or the freelance professions, are still characterised by a continuous increase, a trend which training in the dual system has persistently followed since the eighties.

5.3.4.5 Despite the considerable increase in training positions within the framework of the dual system, in the period from 1975 to 1985 this increase was not alone sufficient to compensate for the over-proportional demand for training in Germany.

The national and state governments therefore felt it necessary to resort to additional *external instruments* from outside the system in order to counter the shortage of training and youth unemployment. Three global strategies may be found:

– bonus programmes,
– employment programmes and
– qualification programmes.

Bonus programmes were (and are again being!) used to attempt to encourage companies to provide additional training places by direct material incentives (= financial bonuses). This practice which is exercised by some Federal states in particular has its own problems since experience suggests it leads to "hitchhiker effects" in companies, i.e. (delayed!) offers of training places which would have been offered anyway without a state subsidy. This practice is therefore only productive under certain conditions.

Employment programmes for young adults or people starting out in a vocation have to date generally been offered by the labour administration in the form of "ABMs" (work procurement measures), i.e. above all financed. This practice also has its problems, since when the funding runs out the beneficiaries are often unemployed (again). Even if ABM labour ends up in permanent employment, generally no new job is created by this[157].

---

157 Cf. Schlegel, W.: Alternative zum "Maßnahmendschungel" – ein kombiniertes Ausbildungs- und Beschäftigungsprogramm für arbeitslose Jugendliche, in: Greinert, W.-D. (Publisher): Lernorte der beruflichen Bildung, Frankfurt/New York 1985, 227-236

Table 23: Supply and demand 1976 to 1993 – equilibrium of supply and demand in the dual system (including new Federal states from 1992 onwards)

	New contracts	Places available	Not placed	Supply	Demand	Supply/demand index	Surplus	Change on previous year Contracts	Change on previous year Supply	Change on previous year Demand
1976	495800	18100	27700	513900	523500	98.2	-9600			
1977	558400	25500	27000	583900	585400	99.7	-1500	12.6	13.6	11.8
1978	601700	22300	23800	624000	625500	99.8	-1500	7.8	6.9	6.9
1979	640300	36900	19700	677200	660000	102.6	17200	6.4	8.5	5.5
1980	650000	44600	17300	694600	667300	104.1	27300	1.5	2.6	1.1
1981	605636	37348	22140	642984	627776	102.4	15208	-6.8	-7.4	-5.9
1982	630990	19995	34180	650985	665170	97.9	-14185	4.2	1.2	6.0
1983	676734	19641	47408	696375	724142	96.2	-27767	7.2	7.0	8.9
1984	705652	21134	58426	726786	764078	95.1	-37292	4.3	4.4	5.5
1985	697089	22021	58905	719110	755994	95.1	-36884	-1.2	-1.1	-1.1
1986	684710	31170	46270	715880	730980	97.9	-15100	-1.8	-0.4	-3.3
1987	645746	44541	33880	690287	679626	101.6	10661	-5.7	-3.6	-7.0
1988	604002	61962	24791	665964	628793	105.9	37171	-6.5	-3.5	-7.5
1989	583736	84913	18278	668649	602014	111.1	66635	-3.4	0.4	-4.3
1990	545562	113873	13969	659435	559531	117.9	99904	-6.5	-1.4	-7.1
1991	539466	128534	11205	668000	550671	121.3	117329	-1.1	1.3	-1.6
Total 1992	**595215**	**126610**	**12975**	**721825**	**608190**	**118.7**	**113635**			
Total 1993[1]	**570093**	**85737**	**17759**	**655830**	**587852**	**111.6**	**67978**	**-4.2**	**-9.1**	**-3.3**
West 1992	**499985**	**123378**	**11756**	**623363**	**511741**	**121.8**	**111622**	**-7.3**	**-6.7**	**-7.1**
West 1993	**470971**	**83655**	**14841**	**554626**	**485812**	**114.2**	**68814**	**-5.8**	**-11.0**	**-5.1**
East 1991[2]	**95230**	**3232**	**1219**	**98462**	**96449**	**102.1**	**2013**			
East 1992[1]	**99122**	**2082**	**2918**	**101204**	**102040**	**99.2**	**-836**	**4.1**	**2.8**	**5.8**

1 The data of newly concluded training contracts in the new Federal states does not include community initiative training places. The number of unplaced applicants has been reduced by 4526, the number of previously unplaced applicants assigned to the community initiative. For this reason both supply and demand are too low in the legal definition.

2 Since no reliable data for the new Federal states is available for 1991, comparison with the previous year's result is not possible.

Source: Vocational Training Reports up to 1993; Federal Institute for Labour, Vocational consultancy statistics, surveyed as at 30 September 1993.

123

The focus of government measures at combating youth unemployment has to date clearly been on *state-subsidised qualification measures*. Already in the 1970s a nationwide network of rehabilitation facilities was set up for socio-political motives and heavily subsidised. The Federal Institute for Labour alone spent around DM 5 billion annually at the time on the operation of this vocational training sector which is an offshoot of the dual system[158].

Then in the 1980s commercial sponsors of the disadvantaged became established. This private sponsor market is still subject to little pedagogic control, and its institutions cannot be classified either as schools or as companies. Some of their efforts are financed by the numerous funds of the European Union (EU) and from the budget of the Federal Institute for Labour (around DM 0.5 bn per year). Although the training offered by this separate vocational training sector is formally associated with the area regulated (Vocational Training Act), the internal structures and principles of the dual system are no longer points of orientation within them[159].

5.3.4.6   It is difficult to get an overview of this private sponsor market; the situation is far from transparent, especially because since the reunification of Germany a multitude of (private) qualification companies have been established in the new Federal states which remove a considerable proportion of the surplus labour from the market or stock it up where the supply of labour is insufficient.

Thus since 1993 a joint initiative has been underway by the Federal government and the new Federal states to encourage up to 10,000 training places with a regional, women's and sector-specific component. DM 500m has been provided for this initiative, 50 % of it from EU funds. This initiative primarily encourages private training establishments and not the construction of the dual system in the new Federal states[160].

---

158 37 "vocational training works" were set up in the old Federal states, with a further DM 800m being spent on an additional 8 in the new Federal states
159 Cf. Biermann, H.: Das Duale System – (k)ein Exportschlager ..., in: Berufsbildung 48 (1994), 2-3, p. 3
160 Cf. Berufsbildungsbericht 1994, p. 160

5.3.5 The utilization function of the dual system of vocational training

The fact that vocational training represents an investment for the future for the economic growth of national economies is today almost universally proclaimed. However, we need to examine whether in the individual case consistent strategies are being followed in this sense in economic and qualification policy. We would guess that this is only rarely the case.

However, it is important for the acceptance of a training system that those interested parties which profit in the long-term from its services can also derive immediate material advantages from vocational training. This applies in particular to the companies as well as to the youth and their parental homes, i.e. social associations and people who do not necessarily orientate their behaviour towards long-term perspectives.

5.3.5.1 In Germany the motivation of companies to offer training places is based on various factors. In the manual trades the vocational tradition which extends back to the Middle Ages undoubtedly still plays a certain role; overall, however, it must be said that the motivation for small and medium-sized businesses to become involved in the training sector is based on the fact that they can make net earnings within the context of the training[161].

In large companies with their overwhelmingly expensive training which is generally remote from production there is another motive for training: the highly-specialised type of qualification of the industrial skilled worker would not even be available on the labour market if industry did not produce him itself. The cost pressure which is today felt by all export-oriented large companies, however, is increasingly making them inclined to move out of this expensive initial training and resort to ''side entrants'' with higher formal qualifications who are then prepared for demanding specialist positions by in-house further training programmes[162]. This trend is coming up against a shrinking of the volume of work in the secondary sector.

---

161 Cf. "Kosten und Finanzierung der außerschulischen Bildung (= Abschlußbericht, Bonn 1974); Bundestagdrucksache VII/1811 of 14.03.1974
162 Cf. footnote 151

The latest cost surveys of vocational training in industry, trade and manual trades are shown in **Table 24** and **Diagram 1**.

5.3.5.2   We have already discussed the emergence of other private sponsor markets in the vocational training sector in section 4.5. In contrast to companies, their training services are generously subsidised. Employers' associations and unions – for different reasons but to the same extent – consider the emergence of a highly-subsidised vocational training sector to be problematic since it could accelerate the current erosion of the dual system still further[163].

5.3.5.3   Under § 10 para. 1 of the Vocational Training Act the trainer must give the trainees "reasonable payment". This is to be gauged according to the age of the employee in such a way that it increases as the vocational training progresses, at least annually. The amount of this "training wage" is generally laid down in the relevant collective agreements, depending on the training vocation to which it belongs. However, the collective agreements contain only minimum amounts which the companies can exceed.

To this extent the training wages differ fairly considerably depending on training vocation and economic region. In the *construction vocations* (scaffolding constructor, bricklayer, joiner, etc.), for example, an average monthly wage of DM 1,399 to DM 1,686 was reached in 1992, whilst in the manual vocation of *gentlemen's tailor* only DM 265 was paid (old Federal states in each case). These differences are due to variations in the financial strength of the sectors, to the more or less successful representation of interest by the unions and to disequilibrium of supply and demand in the training and skilled labour markets.

The average training wage per month in 1993 is shown by training area in **Diagram 2**. The trend in the average training remuneration between 1976 and 1993 is shown in **Diagram 3**.

---

163 Cf. Berufsbildungsbericht 1994. Hauptausschuß des Bundesinstituts nimmt Stellung zum Entwurf, Pressemitteilung des BiBB 7/94, dated 3.03.94

5.3.5.4   The German training system, the present structure of wich began to develop around 100 years ago, is a prime example of the role of vocational training as a factor in economic and social modernisation. Whilst in its initial development phase (approx. 1870-1920) the focus was particulary on the social integration of lower middle class (male) youth into the recently established bourgeois national state, from the twenties onwards vocational training gradually became regarded as a factor of pruduction, primarily by industry, and was given a particular form of organisation.This interpretation remains today; in fact, the emergence of the ''training economy'' has reinforced the tendency to regard training and education as economic and socio-political modernisation factors. The final report of the Enquête Commission on ''Training 2000'' which the German Bundestag initiated in 1987 expressly emphasised the opinion shared by all parties and experts of the importance of training and (vocational) training with regard to social cohesion, democracy, encouragement of the individual, the *securing of wealth*, improvements in living and working conditions and nature conservation[164].

5.3.5.5   In this respect it is again recommended that we first look back at the beginnings of the dual system in the 19th century. The political programme of economic stabilisation of the old middle class – above all the manual trades – expressly included the reorganisation of vocational training within the framework of trade and industry legislation. The other components consisted of the ordered construction of self-administering bodies for manual trades (chambers, guilds) and title protection for the *master craftsman's examination*. Even today in Germany the unity of the vocational organisation of the manual trades and vocational training for these trades is secured in a special ''Craftsmen's Order'' (HWO).

This means that in Germany vocational training with binding regulations is considered to be one of the central principles which allows the economic existence of small and medium-sized companies in particular. Consequently the promotion of vocational training plays an important role in the programmes for the reconstruction of medium-sized businesses in the new Federal states. Central measures are: the construction of industry-wide

---

164   Cf. Schlußbericht der Enquête-Kommission ''Zukünftige Bildungspolitik – Bildung 2000'', Bundestagsdrucksache 11/7820 dated 05.09.1990

Table 24: Costs of in-company vocational training 1991 – averages per trainee and year according to company size

Cost types	Overall average		Averages by company size							
			1 to 9 employees		10 to 49 employees		50 to 499 employees		500 or more employees	
	in DM	as % of gross costs	in DM	as % of gross costs	in DM	as % of gross costs	in DM	as % of gross costs	in DM	as % of gross costs
Gross costs	29573	100.0	27473	100.0	28176	100.0	30344	100.0	35692	100.0
Earnings	11711	39.6	12221	44.5	11465	40.7	12100	39.9	10311	28.9
Net costs	17862	60.4	15252	55.5	16711	59.3	18245	60.1	25381	71.1
Staff costs of trainees	14435	48.8	12336	44.9	13562	48.1	15827	52.2	15833	44.4
of which: training wages	10329	34.9	9087	33.1	9793	34.8	11170	36.8	11167	31.3
Costs of training personnel	11652	39.4	11943	43.5	11799	41.9	10973	36.2	13332	37.4
Material and fixed costs	1048	3.5	313	1.1	534	1.9	1058	3.5	4362	12.2
Other costs	2438	8.2	2880	10.5	2281	8.1	2486	8.2	2164	6.1

Source: Federal Institute for Vocational Training

Source: Vocational Training Report 1994, page 103

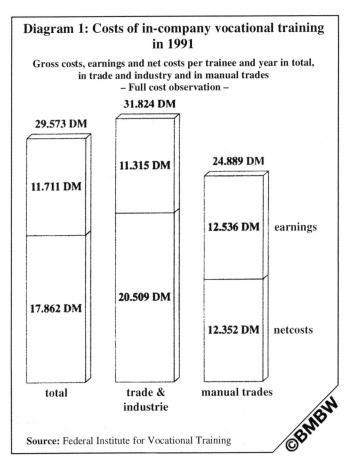

Diagram 1: Costs of in-company vocational training in 1991

Gross costs, earnings and net costs per trainee and year in total, in trade and industry and in manual trades
– Full cost observation –

29.573 DM
31.824 DM

11.711 DM
11.315 DM
24.889 DM

12.536 DM   earnings

17.862 DM
20.509 DM

12.352 DM   netcosts

total
trade & industrie
manual trades

©BMBW

Source: Federal Institute for Vocational Training

Source: Vocational Training Report 1994, page 102

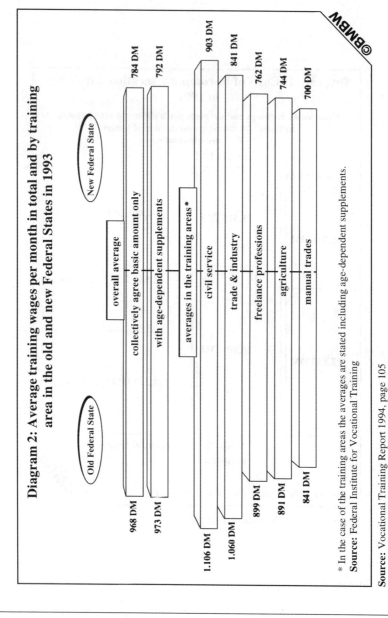

Diagram 2: Average training wages per month in total and by training area in the old and new Federal States in 1993

Old Federal State | New Federal State

overall average

collectively agree basic amount only — 968 DM / 784 DM

with age-dependent supplements — 973 DM / 792 DM

averages in the training areas *

civil service — 1.106 DM / 903 DM

trade & industry — 1.060 DM / 841 DM

freelance professions — 899 DM / 762 DM

agriculture — 891 DM / 744 DM

manual trades — 841 DM / 700 DM

©BMBW

* In the case of the training areas the averages are stated including age-dependent supplements.
Source: Federal Institute for Vocational Training

Source: Vocational Training Report 1994, page 105

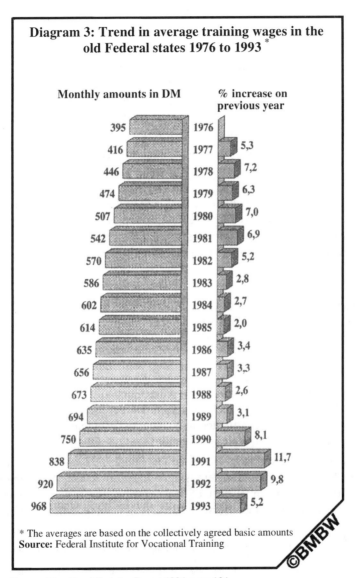

Diagram 3: Trend in average training wages in the old Federal states 1976 to 1993 [*]

Monthly amounts in DM

% increase on previous year

Monthly amounts in DM	Year	% increase on previous year
395	1976	
416	1977	5,3
446	1978	7,2
474	1979	6,3
507	1980	7,0
542	1981	6,9
570	1982	5,2
586	1983	2,8
602	1984	2,7
614	1985	2,0
635	1986	3,4
656	1987	3,3
673	1988	2,6
694	1989	3,1
750	1990	8,1
838	1991	11,7
920	1992	9,8
968	1993	5,2

* The averages are based on the collectively agreed basic amounts
Source: Federal Institute for Vocational Training

©BMBW

Source: Vocational Training Report 1994, page 104

131

vocational training centres, the delegation of experienced training consultants from the west and subsidisation of company and industry-wide training places from public budgets.

Otherwise a number of training place initiatives were passed by the Federal German cabinet generally within the framework of the "Upturn – East" co-operative project (resolution of 24.04.91). The economic structural change required in the new Federal states is supported by an extensive further training campaign. In this connection the funds of the "Work Promotion Act" for the support of vocational further training, retraining or commercial orientation were given a substantial top-up (to a total of DM 6.8 bn in 1991).

5.3.5.6   Today it has become usual to add to the comparative criteria for the economic competitiveness of a country – productivity of labour, service-readiness and labour and wage legislation – the training status of the workforce, for which the existing vocational training system is crucially decisive[165].

Today in the international discussion of the training models which may be considered the most efficient, vocational training systems in which the training services of the companies play a central role have emerged as "best solutions"[166].

Of the three basic models of institutionalised vocational training – the market model, bureaucratic model and dual model – the market model and the dual systems would be estimated to be the most efficient.

If we compare the advantages and disadvantages of these two models we find that the German dual system is a *strategically-oriented training model*[167]. Its advantage in respect of the securing of permanent economic growth consists in the fact that with its aid long-term qualification potential

---

165 Cf. Zedler, R.: Standortvorteil: Berufsausbildung in: Lenske, W. (Publisher): Qualified in Germany, Cologne 1988, 75-98, p. 75 f.
166 Cf. Vocational and Technical Education and Training: A World Bank Policy Paper, Washington D.C. 1991
167 Cf. Zedler, loc. cit. p. 95

can be built up. Its weakness is its bureaucratic structure, although this is far less than in the state area, and the associated lack of flexibility in respect of technical and social modernisation thrusts.

Market models of vocational training, such as in Japan or the USA, are on the other hand in a position to react very quickly to changes in requirements. In the terminology we have chosen they may be described as *tactically-oriented training models*. Their disadvantage is that the qualification potential built up tends to satisfy only short-term requirements; it is not rooted in the framework of a handed down vocation of work[168].

5.3.6 The integration function of the dual system of vocational training

German vocational pedagogics has referred time and again – whether positively or critically – to the fact that vocational training does not simply impart technical qualifications but should also integrate the trainees into society and generate loyalty potential to the determining socio-economic and political system. In the international discussion this understanding of vocational training policy as targeted social policy often meets with widespread misunderstanding or rejection.

This task is almost exclusively assigned to the general school system, although insight and experience suggest that vocational training and vocational practice have a much greater socialisation potential than cognitive learning.

5.3.6.1   The fact that vocational training not only imparts technical qualifications but also social and political orientations which encourage social cohesion may be described as something of a "German philosophy". The fact that this view is not very widespread is related in part to the fact that in many countries technical and vocational training is not given the status of *education*. Vocational training courses in these countries are accordingly often organised along narrow lines and not very intellectually demanding.

---

168 Cf. Georg, W.: Berufliche Bildung des Auslands: Japan, Baden-Baden 1993; Lauglo, J.: Vocational training: analysis of policies and modes. Case studies of Sweden, Germany and Japan, (=International Institute for Educational Planning, UNESCO), Paris 1993

A progressive understanding of education assumes that equipping individuals to cope with specific situations in life can be achieved by both theoretical and practically oriented learning processes. The practically oriented learning processes must not consist only of learning specialised vocational skills (one man, one skill).

The concept of the German skilled worker or skilled labour training excludes such constrictions from the start. From the outset it implies relatively broad training in technical terms alone, supplemented with theoretical and also general cultural aspects by a public school (= vocational school). In the case of the training vocations which have been reorganised since the 1970s the level of qualification realised has been still higher: the aim is the *vocational capacity to act* in the sense of independent planning, execution and checking of tasks. It is therefore a concept of qualification which includes technical, social and personal skills. The staged qualification programme which aims for flexible, wide-ranging basic vocations is here often conveyed by training methods which are far superior to traditional scholastic methods[169].

5.3.6.2   Despite the flexibility of the training system and despite a variety of measures and programmes, some of the youth remain without vocational training. In Germany this proportion is currently around 10 % of an age group. The basic reasons for not taking up vocational training or not completing it successfully are a deficit in primary and/or general scholastic socialisation or the weaknesses of the person himself.

For these *disadvantaged youths* there are differentiated forms of measures to prepare for a vocation and assistance accompanying training which are financed by the Federal Institute for Labour within the context of the "Labour Promotion Act" (AFG). In 1991 measures for 60,000 people were supported in the old Federal states within the framework of vocational training for disadvantaged trainees (§ 40c AFG). Here a distinction is made between two categories of target groups:

---

169 Cf. e.g. Klein, U.: PETRA. Projekt- und transferorientierte Ausbildung, 2nd edition Berlin/ Munich 1990

- AFG § 40c (2):original target group (learning-impaired German youth, socially disadvantaged youth, foreign youth); this is a support instrument *independent of the labour market*;
- AFG § 40c (4):expanded target group (unplaced training applicants, known as "bankrupt apprentices"); this is a support instrument *dependent on the labour market* and having a time limit.

5.3.6.3   The encouragement of *vocational training for the disabled* is made possible both with the support of the labour administration and in special training courses via §§ 48 VTA/§ 42 b HWO. According to the statistics of the Federal Institute for Labour concerning vocational rehabilitation, 13,672 disabled persons began training in recognised training vocations (§ 25 VTA) in the reporting year of 1990/91; 4077 began a special form of training in accordance with §§ 48 VTA/42 b HWO. Of these around 56 % were trained in companies, 21 % in special "vocational further training works" and 23 % in other establishments (e.g. "protected" workshops).

5.3.6.4   There are also specific programmes in Germany for the *vocational rehabilitation of adults*. People in employment who can no longer carry on their trained or previously practised vocation due to illness or accident are trained in further training or retraining schemes largely according to the principle of "rehabilitation rather than pension". At the end of 1990 9,030 rehabilitating adults were on further training schemes in the old Federal states and 31,833 on retraining schemes. 85 % of those in rehabilitation were assisted by the Federal Institute for Labour and 12 % by pension or accident insurance.

5.3.6.5   In public opinion, and probably not only in Germany, there is a persistent conception of a direct correlation between unemployment and (youth) criminality. This theory has been contested in scientific circles for some time and has led to a variety of differentiations.

The current prevailing scientific opinion is that the emergence of (youth) criminality is caused by other, weightier factors than unemployment. However, unemployment undoubtedly marks a reinforcing factor in the disposition of youths to criminality. Two groups seem to be particularly conspicuous: long-term unemployed youths and those who become unemployed immediately after leaving school[170].

In Germany youth unemployment – particularly since the 1920s – is always felt to be a factor in social destabilisation and therefore understood as a political challenge. Vocational training programmes regularly play the prominent role in the measures taken to combat it. When the limits of the capacity of the established training system were reached – most recently in 1975-85 – additional vocational training courses were provided by governmental, semi-governmental and private (publicly financed) providers to a considerable extent, in order largely to save school-leavers in particular from the negative experiences of being out of work. Using these measures the majority of the youth threatened by unemployment were able to be integrated into the work process.

5.3.6.6   For historical/structural reasons vocation is a central intermediary element of social relationships, i.e. its "role nature" is given constitutive significance for building up and regulating relationships between the members of a society. To this extent the development of the self-identity of individuals is closely associated with taking on specific vocational roles[171].

The extent to which a vocational training system contributes to the initiation or support of such identity-forming processes is difficult to measure in principle. The first thing of significance is probably whether the self-reflection of a system becomes a problem, i.e. whether institutional structures are developed within its framework which allow analytical access to the effects outlined above.

A special pedagogic discipline – vocational pedagogics – has emerged in the course of the development of the German dual vocational training system, within the context of which initially speculative but now increasingly empirical corresponding characterisation processes of vocational training and practice were and are captured and analyzed. The initial results of such

---

170 Cf. Hermanns, M.: Jugendarbeitslosigkeit seit der Weimarer Republik, Opladen 1990
171 Cf. Beck, U./M. Brater/H. Daheim: Soziologie der Arbeit und der Berufe, Reinbek 1980, p. 215 ff.

"vocational socialisation research" lead us to conclude that different training arrangements also have specific effects on the social consciousness and character formation of trainees[172].

---

172 Cf. Lempert, W.: Sozialisation in der betrieblichen Ausbildung. Der Beitrag der Lehre zur Entwicklung sozialer Orientierungen im Spiegel neuer Längsschnittuntersuchungen, in: Thomas, H./G. Elstermann (Publisher): Bildung und Beruf, Berlin/Heidelberg/New York/Tokyo 1986, 105-144; Hoff, E.-H./W. Lempert/L. Lappe: Persönlichkeitsentwicklung in Facharbeiterbiographien, Bern/Stuttgart/Toronto 1991

5.4 The outlook for the dual system of vocational training in Germany

In the current discussion on the future of Germany as an economic location the fear has often been expressed that the continued existence of the dual system of vocational training is at risk even in the medium term, despite the high regard in which it is held. It has been noted that already in the 1992 training year the major west German industrial companies in particular began to restrict their training capacity; this trend has continued in 1993[173].

Surveys indicate that the reasons for this exit of industry from the dual system are not only related to the economy but also to structural factors: the volume of work in the manufacturing sector is shrinking and there are already sufficient numbers of qualified applicants – technical college graduates and graduates of vocational academies – on the labour market who require only low-cost training in the company[174].

Should this withdrawal of industry from the dual system of initial training persist as is feared, the dual system of vocational training will be in serious danger of becoming a residual qualification factor similar to the lower school. Since the 1930s at least training as a skilled industrial worker has been the core and measure of the "German system" of vocational training. Even a superficial look back at history shows that practically all the innovations and all the productive initiatives for further development and adaptation of the system to technical progress originated on the part of industry[175].

The increasing withdrawal of traditional groups of applicants from dual vocational training is regarded as a second central crisis phenomenon. Whilst in 1982 473 people completed dual vocational training for every 100 university graduates, 10 years later the number was down to 255. The reverse in the trend in the training sector signalled by these figures became widely felt amongst the public in 1990 when the number of those studying at

---

173 Cf. Berufsbildungsbericht 1994, p. 4 f.
174 Cf. Bardeleben, R. v. et al: Kosten und Nutzen der betrieblichen Berufsausbildung, in: Berufsbildung in Wissenschaft und Praxis 23 (1994), p. 3-12
175 Cf. Greinert, W.-D.: Das "deutsche System" der Berufsausbildung. Geschichte, Organisation, Perspektiven, Baden-Baden 1993, p. 61 ff.

universities exceeded the number training in the dual system for the first time [176].

Whether the increased preference of "state full-time training forms" (employers associations) corresponds to the recognisable development of need in the employment system is doubtful. What is certain is that this "voting with their feet" by the new generation of youth is based on entirely rational criteria. Until now university graduates had markedly higher income expectations than those completing the dual system; they were subject to much lower employment risks – until now! – and obtained considerably more job satisfaction. This is related in particular to the fact that their further training and promotion opportunities are far better than those of the clientele of dual training[177]. Thus despite all the efforts at reform in the past 25 years, Germany still has two clearly unequal privileged paths of training, and now everyone understands that.

The tougher selection and displacement competition in the dual system is a further central symptom of the crisis. This is felt rather more indirectly, e.g. via the rising drop-out rates, but marks a crucial negative trend. To the same extent that the dual system lost its clear qualification function for gifted Volkschule and Hauptschule (lower school) leavers ("the best sons of the people": B. Lutz), internal selection and displacement processes are increasing. Today the equivalent of "A" level students tend to occupy the demanding training places in the commercial and services sector; the capacity not taken up by them is taken by intermediate school leavers. Lower school leavers tend to take up manufacturing vocations in industry and manual trades, whilst special students, school drop-outs and other peripheral groups have to make do with the unattractive service and manual trade vocations or their training places[178]. This type of restricted vocational choice – the worst training places for the weakest! – gradually leads to incorrect orientations and frustration. This is visible in the increase in the drop-out rates: almost one in four people beginning training now drops out and the drop-out rates in manual trades are markedly above the average[179]. The second effect is that potential skilled workers which the private sector

176 Cf. Berufsbildungsbericht 1994, p. 23
177 Cf. Alex, L./U. Landsberg: Forschungsseminar zu den Herausforderungen an die duale Ausbildung, in: Berufsbildung in Wissenschaft und Praxis 22 (1993), 28-31, p. 29
178 f. Berufsbildungsbericht 1994, p. 61 ff.
179 Ditto, p. 72 f.

would also make available as labour are pushed out by those holding certificates who then generally leave the vocation after training.

This type of mismanagement and an increasing number of school and training failures are the logical consequence of a training and vocational training system which is increasingly oriented towards "meritocratic" principles. The social consequences are foreseeable: on the one hand, an increasing shortage of skilled labour, and on the other an army of non-integrated or non-integrable people.

5.4.1 An abundance of offers:
The competing interpretations of the crisis

Whilst there is broad agreement on the crisis phenomena in the now heated discussion, great differences of opinion are found amongst the research into the causes. Logically this results in differing estimations of the future of the dual system and the promising routes out of the crisis.

To summarize the arguments of the "pessimists", i.e. those predicting an imminent end to the dual system, there are four central reasons for taking this view:

1. The process of shrinkage in the potential for socially organised work associated with a "de-traditionalising and de-standardisation of the working world" which can be seen is liquidating the classical vocation model and thus also the necessity for systematic vocational training.
2. The increasing tendency of modern societies to generate and legitimise social inequality principally via the training qualifications of *general schools* (= "meritocratic" principle) is forcing a general training competition for certificates which promise privilege which can only be given by grammar schools and university.
3. The undoubted shift in emphasis within vocational training from initial training to further training is forcing a devaluation of the dual training system as an allocation agency of corporate status and vocational prestige.
4. The progression of the internal European market is modifying the significance of the "German" (dual) training system and its work organisation basis: the state-sanctioned skilled worker status. Scholastic and

140

market-orientedtraining models are entering into fierce competition with training organised along dual lines[180].

In a critical appreciation of these reasons one cannot help concluding that they are all founded on an empirically weak basis.

1. A forthcoming end to the vocational organisation of labour has been consistently prophesied since the beginning of the new age. "Critical" vocational pedagogics since the time of Anna Siemsen and Erna Barschak has also flogged this thesis. However, to date there is no alternative in sight to our traditional system of socially organised work. What is without doubt is that there are far-reaching processes of change in the relationship between work and vocation and science is having difficulty capturing these reasonably and interpreting them. To this extent the repeated forecasts of the end of the working and vocational society are not only false but they do not belong amongst "tried and tested forecasts"[181].

2. The increasing evolution of "meritocratic logic" in developed societies and training systems does not mark a compulsory trend. There are still some countries in Europe other than Germany in which the "meritocratic vicious circle" (B. Lutz) with its symptoms of high youth unemployment, a flood of academics with a simultaneous shortage of skilled labour has not yet been able to develop (Switzerland, the Netherlands, Austria, Denmark). These are countries in which learning is again reliably institutionalised in vocational practice. As comparative training research shows, meritocratic tendencies can also be controlled politically to a certain extent[182].

3. The fact that further training or readiness for further training is increasingly determining the careers of individuals is indisputable. However, it is questionable whether vocational further training based only on theo-

---

180 Cf. e.g. Geißler, K.A.: Perspektiven der Weiterentwicklung des Systems der dualen Berufsausbildung in der Bundesrepublik, in: Bundesinstitut für Berufsbildung (Publisher): Die Rolle der beruflichen Bildung und Berufsbildungsforschung im internationalen Vergleich, Berlin/Bonn 1991, 101-110

181 Cf. Hesse, H.A.: Wandel der Berufe – Ende der Qualifikationen?, in: arbeiten + lernen 3 (1981), 18, 9-12

182 Cf. Lutz, B.: Herausforderungen an eine zukunftsorientierte Berufsbildungspolitik, in: Bundesinstitut für Berufsbildung (Publisher): Die Rolle der beruflichen Bildung und Berufsbildungsforschung im internationalen Vergleich, Berlin/Bonn 1991, 27-36

retical abstract training courses is sufficient to satisfy the complex needs of the modern working world. All our experience suggests not; the assault by "A" level students on the dual system is probably to be interpreted not least as a critical vote against a general basic training which is remote from practice. This means that vocational initial training will continue to represent a not sufficient but necessary qualification phase in the future[183].

4. The argument that the "German system" of vocational training could be subject to international competition can hardly be upheld in view of the widespread interest in the model. On the contrary: two important EU countries (France and the UK) have in recent years made efforts to organised parts of their training along dual lines. The fact that these efforts have had little success is another matter. In the international discussion on vocational training scholastic training models are no longer considered feasible. Training systems with company participation are considered "best" solutions, and the "German system" (a state-managed market model) essentially as an ideal type[184].

The "optimists", i.e. those who continue to give the dual system a chance of survival, associate this way of thinking less with research into the causes and more with proposals for more or less fundamental reform measures. Two groups may be distinguished: one believes that the desired stabilisation can be achieved by internal corrections whilst the other advocates radical changes which go beyond the framework of the dual system.

The guiding aims are:

1. opening up of the dual system to previously disadvantaged groups,
2. increasing its attractiveness compared with grammar school and study and
3. the first group claims the vocational training will be "fit for Europe" following concrete reform proposals: differentiation of vocational training according to previous education of trainees, programmes for the specially gifted and disadvantaged, increasing the quality of training in school and in the company through innovative learning schemes (action

---

183 Cf. Voigt, W.: Berufliche Weiterbildung. Eine Einführung, Munich 1986, p. 113 ff.
184 Cf. World Bank: Vocational and technical education and training. A world bank policy paper. Washington D.C. 1991

orientation, communication of key qualifications, etc.), massive encouragement of vocational further training, opening up of technical colleges and universities to technically qualified persons without "A" levels, linking of company training to technical college training, compulsory introduction of foreign language teaching in vocational training and exchange programmes for trainees and those beginning a vocation[185].

The group of radical reformers regards this programme as rather cosmetic and makes instead three far-reaching core demands in return for which it promises different training behaviour amongst the incoming youth:

1. Revision of civil service legislation with the aim of removing the traditional privilege granted to the academic vocations. They expect this measure would also send marked signals to the private sector regarding wages policy.
2. Building up an attractive system of vocational promotion opportunities in all economic sectors. It is claimed that these career paths would have to be institutionally linked with a legally secured system of vocational further training. Initial training and further training are also to be linked organisationally and in terms of content.
3. The creation of integrated training courses at secondary stage II in an act which also allows university entrance qualifications to be obtained. Thus it is a matter of realising double-qualifying training paths on the basis of qualified vocational training in accordance with the Vocational Training Act. Moreover, it is a matter of dissolvingthe long form of the grammar school, i.e. consistent grading of general school training with genuine choices after 10th grade[186].

A critical appreciation of the programme starting points of the two groups of reformers can be given briefly: the proposals by the moderates would not lead us to expect any decisive changes in the crisis situation of the dual system, whilst the demands of the radicals have no change of being realised, not even in part.

---

185 Cf. e.g. Berufsbildungsbericht 1994, p. 2 and 8 f.
186 Cf. e.g. Greinert, W.-D: Berufsausbildung und sozio-ökomonischer Wandel, in: Zeitschrift für Pädagogik 40 (1994), 357-172, p. 370

5.4.2 Expansion of training and missed reforms: The real causes of the crisis

The false estimations of the possible outlook for the development of the dual system of vocational training in Germany outlined above are undoubtedly based on a faulty research into the causes of its current crisis situation. if we orientate ourselves towards previous political models we need to make a clear distinction between two fields of causes, namely:

1. between the objective problem, i.e. that brought about by non-wilful or uncontrolled factors, and
2. the failures of politics induced specifically for the interests concerned[187].

The objective problem is marked in our opinion by three trends in the training and employment system which more or less compulsorily result in an industrial society in global competition from a long-term development perspective. These are:

1. Shrinking volume of work in the secondary (= manufacturing) sector. Both developments which can already be observed and long-term needs projections confirm a continuous trend towards shifting activity structures in the employment system: production and primary service activities are becoming less significant quantitatively as well as qualitatively and instead strong employment gains are being made by what is known as the "secondary" service activities. Thus the IAB forecast projection of 1989 assumes that in the period from 1987 to 2010 (upper growth variant) there will be a loss of over 12 % of jobs in manufacturing activities and 8% in the area of primary service activities. This decline in employment will however probably be more than compensated for by the expansion in secondary services (+62.5 %!)[188].

The background to this development is formed by global competitive pressures and rationalisation initiatives based on new technologies which force changes in both employment and labour organisation.

---

187 Cf. Offe, C.: Berufsbildungsreform. Eine Fallstudie über Reformpolitik, Frankfurt a.M. 1975
188 Cf. Tessaring, M.: Das duale System der Berufsausbildung in Deutschland: Attraktivität und Beschäftigungsperspektiven, in: Mitteilungen aus der Arbeitsmarkt- und Berufsforschung 26 (1993), 131-161, p. 155

2. Demographic quantitative developments and the competition of the training paths. The dual system of vocational training reached the peak of its absorptive ability in the mid 1980s and since then new admissions and numbers of those completing the training have fallen drastically.the reason for this fall is primarily the demographic trend: the pressure of the baby boom years declined considerably after 1986; the dual system must adjust to falling numbers of applicants and the employment system to a smaller potential of trained skilled labour. However, this situation will deteriorate still further in the long-term: the consolidation phase after the turn of the century will be followed by a fall in the numbers of 16-19 year olds which will be considerably greater than that of the 1980s[189].

However, the quantitative decline in the number of trainees in the dual system is only partly due to demographic factors; a second reason is that the social demand for training in this area of qualification has declined considerably. Strictly bounded off from the general training system for decades in terms of entitlement policy, organisation and curriculum, the dual system is today in fierce competition with the academic path of training.

3. Great changes in training behaviour of broad strata of the population. Whilst in 1960 three quarters of all leavers of the general schools came from the lower school or Volkschule (9 % with ''A'' level equivalents, 16 % with ''O'' level equivalents) the proportion of lower school leavers (with and without a leaving certificate) had fallen by 1991 to 38 %, whilst the proportion of ''A'' level students had risen to 27 % and ''O'' level students to 35 %. The structural changes seem even greater if we also take into account the leaving certificates or entitlements obtained at the vocational schools: then the proportion of those with a university qualification increases to 34 % and lower school leavers falls to 31 %. According to relevant surveys, this trend towards higher school leaving qualifications has far from been broken[190].

The changed training behaviour is due to the lapse of traditional structures which for a long time stabilised the training and vocational choice behav-

---

189 Ditto, p. 137 ff.
190 Ditto, p. 137; cf. also Alex, L.: Veränderung des Bildungsverhaltens in Deutschland, in: Berufsbildung in Wissenschaft und Praxis 23 (1994), 43-45

iour of large groups of the population, but by the early 1970s at least had been removed by socio-economic modernisation impulses.

Let us remember: immediately after the Second World War training systems could still be identified in all western European countries which had emerged from a long development process lasting around 150 years and essentially had very similar features: for around 90 % of an age group compulsory full-time schooling ended at age 13 or 14 and only a minority (the children of the privileged upper classes) attended middle and higher schools. Some of these students (around 5-8 % of an age group on average in western Europe in the 1950/51 academic year) then studied at university, not all of them graduating. Only around 4-6 % of an age group graduated and embarked upon working life with this formal qualification[191].

In the early fifties the education sector began to expand in western European countries; indicators of the quantitative expansion of "higher" training courses in particular increase with sometimes enormous growth rates. Thus, for example, the proportion of an age group starting university increased between 1950 and 1970 from 6.2 % to 15.4 % in the Federal Republic of Germany, from 8.5 % to 28.5 % in France and from 6.0 % to 37.6 % in Sweden[192]. In the Federal Republic of Germany this spectacular rise in attendance of grammar school and university has since the mid sixties been accompanied by a passionate public debate on the "German education catastrophe"[193] in which the backwardness of training development in the Federal Republic compared with comparable industrial nations is pointed out and judged to be a failure of education policy which threatens the future.

The structural changes implemented on the basis of this debate and the political pressure which it generated in the 1970s in the (west) German education system aimed to expand access to universities in particular. Nonetheless, at the end of the sixties the vocational training sector in the Federal Republic was caught up in the whirlpool of reform discussion. This initially peaked in the arguments concerning the Vocational Training Act (1969)

---

191 Cf. Lutz, B.: Die Interdependenz von Bildung und Beschäftigung und das Problem der Erklärung der Bildungsexpansion, in: Sozialer Wandel in Westeuropa. Verhandlungen des 19. Deutschen Soziologentages, published by J. Matthes, Frankfurt/New York 1979, 634-670
192 Ditto, p. 637
193 Cf. Picht, G.: Die deutsche Bildungskatastrophe, 1st edition Freiburg 1964

and the recommendation by the German Education Council in the same year entitled "Improvement of Apprenticeship Training"[194]; the second was in 1973/74 when the so-called "marker points" of the Federal government were published in a new version of the Vocational Training Act and with the secondary stage recommendation from the Education Council[195].

One explanation for this development is given by *Burkart Lutz*. After Lutz had rejected attempts at interpreting the German expansion of training as far too narrow in 1979, he succeeded in 1984 in his spectacular investigation "The brief dream of permanent prosperity" in giving a conclusive explanation for the driving forces of the European training expansion after the war - and thus also for the crisis in the dual system[196].

In his analysis Lutz declared a central feature of European economic development up to the 1950s to be the existence of an economic dualism, i.e. the co-existence of a modern industrial market economy sector and a traditional economic sector (cottage industries, manual trades, retail trade and primary services, domestic science). The particular exchange relationships between these two economic sectors and the behavioural logic determining them was formed (according to Lutz) by a mechanism of "positive coupling" with prosperity effects which in Europe until the beginning of the First World War were, however, dependent on the primary impulse of growing exports and imperialistic expansion. "At the moment when the export economy comes to a permanent standstill," Lutz wrote, "the same mechanism of positive coupling results in a "depression spiral"[197].

More recent economic history regards the period between 1914 and 1945-50 as a phase of general stocking up of economic development, including in Europe; a long-lasting period of stagnation. This was not always equally marked in the various industrial countries of Europe and was also interrupted by the armaments boom of the thirties; in comparison to this crisis peri-

194 Deutscher Bildungsrat. Empfehlungen der Bildungskommission: Zur Verbesserung der Lehrlingsausbildung, (Bonn 1969)
195 Printed at Pätzold, G. (Publisher): Quellen und Dokumente zur Geschichte des Berufsbildungsgesetzes, loc. cit, p. 255-261; Deutscher Bildungsrat. Empfehlungen der Bildungskommission: Zur Neuordnung der Sekundarstufe II. Konzept für eine Verbindung von allgemeinem und beruflichem Lernen, (Bonn 1974)
196 Lutz, B.: Der kurze Traum immerwährender Prosperität, Frankfurt/New York 1984
197 Ditto, p. 174 and p. 113

od however, the USA experienced a development between 1914 and 1930 representing uninterrupted continuation of prosperity which we had here in Europe before and after the turn of the centuryand after overcoming the "Great Depression"[198].

In the period following the Second World War, or more precisely from the 1950s onwards, Lutz finds two central components which form the basis of the astonishing development of prosperity in the industrial countries of Europe: state welfare policy, in particular the neutralisation of the wages act, and – following the associated dismissal of the "reserve army" mechanism – the annexing and absorption of the traditional economic sector by the industrial market economy sector. In this theory the overcoming of economic duality is the supporting impulse of the post-war prosperity in Europe, as a basis for mass wealth and new mass culture or a "new way of living" (Lutz).

There are various consequences of this development; what is interesting in relation to our question is that along with the traditional sector its stabilising influence on the training and vocational choice behaviour of large groups of the population also disappeared. It was increasingly recognised that access to the privileged positions in the economy and society was exclusively via grammar school and university, that only "higher education" offered a guarantee of being given above-average social opportunities.

The evening out of ways of living of almost all groups of the population associated with the growth in prosperity, unprecedented in history, placed the remaining forms and causes of unequal opportunities in life into the public consciousness with unusual clarity[199]; the reduction or legitimation of these became a political problem. In Lutz's opinion, the reform of the traditional education system in which it was believed that one of the major causes of the uneven distribution of social opportunities had been found offered the best opportunity for criticism of the social inequality which existed without risking breaking down the established power and interest structures.

The vocational training system in (west) Germany faced this criticism in two respects: firstly, there was now widespread awareness amongst the

---

198 Ditto, p. 79 ff.
199 Lutz, Die Interdependenz von Bildung und Beschäftigung, loc. cit., p. 654 ff.

public that the traditional split in the German training system between "general education" and "vocational training" was a pronounced sign of division into social classes. The old verdict of August Bebel that "general education is the vocational training of the rulers, vocational training is the general education of the ruled" then became a familiar quotation[200]. The removal of the pedagogic, organisational and curricular differences between the two training sectors, the "integration of general and vocational training", was thus one of the core demands in the public debate on education[201].

The second critical objection to the dual vocational training system was directed towards its lack of qualification ability. The traditional economic sector, for the limited technological and work-organisational dimension of which the existing vocational training system had been designed around 1900, had evaporated; the technological and economic adaptation of the manual trades, trade, farming and domestic science to the industrial market economy sector made greater demands of the qualificationswith which the workforce employed there had to be equipped, but which the training practice which had emerged was unable to provide. As numerous empirical surveys from the early seventies undoubtedly demonstrate, it had largely become a simple instrument of exploitation[202], a training reality with shortcomings, against which even those affected themselves rose up in a spontaneous and autonomous "apprentice movement"[203].

The doubly motivated attack on the dual system which peaked in the early seventies generated a political pressure which initially nobody dared to oppose, even the employers. The consequence was an abundance of proposals and plans for massive intervention in the established training system, but the chances of realising these were largely destroyed by the global econom-

---

200 The then president of the Education and Science Union, Erich Frister, particularly contributed to the revival of Bebel's saying.
201 As a prominent document cf. the secondary stage recommendation by the German Educational Council (Deutscher Bildungsrat) (footnote 195).
202 Cf. by way of summary: Stratmann, K.: Berufsausbildung auf dem Prüfstand: Zur These vom "bedauerlichen Einzelfall". Ergebnisse empirischer Untersuchungen zur Situation der Berufsbildung in der Bundesrepublik, in: Zeitschrift für Pädagogik 19 (1973), 731-758
203 Cf. Haug, H.-J./H. Maessen: Was wollen die Lehrlinge?, Frankfurt a.M./Hamburg 1971; Weiler, J./R. Freitag: Ausbildung statt Ausbeutung. Der Kampf der Essener Lehrlinge, Reinbek 1971

ic crisis which set in in 1974 and the threatening "training catastrophe" – the increasing demand for training places with a decline in supply.

The global economic crisis and training place supply crisis thus provided the dual system with a reprieve from reform in the seventies, resulting in a fatal misjudgement by the competent education politicians, the social partners and the Federal government: it was thought that a further rationalisation of the system would be sufficient and the required fundamental reforms were rejected. Since the beginning of the nineties, because lower birth rate years are now allowing students to move relatively freely in the existing training institutions, "meritocratic logic" (Lutz) has been evolving freely. This means that vocational positions, even in the non-academic sector, are increasingly assigned on the basis of school results and certificates. The side entrant is pushing out the skilled worker[204].

5.4.3 The question at the root of training policy: Does the dual system of vocational training have to be maintained?

Now we can naturally ask whether the dual system actually has to be rescued at all. After all, there are very different training systems, such as that in Japan, which do not recognise any vocations in the sense in which we use the term and have no state regulated training for these. Yet nobody would dispute that the Japanese are extraordinarily successful in economic terms. So does Germany need the dual system of vocational training?

In our view this question must be answered in the affirmative, essentially for two reasons. The first reason is an economic reason or a reason of economic policy. Our system of production (including to a certain extent our system of services) is based in terms of labour organisation on the principle of skilled labour, i.e. our organisation of labour essentially has three levels: the skilled worker forms the basis and is followed by the master craftsman and engineer levels. In other countries, including in Europe, there are substantially more levels to their labour organisation, above all more supervi-

---

204 Cf. e.g. Drexel, I.: Das Ende des Facharbeiteraufstiegs? Neue mittlere Bildungs- und Karrierewege in Deutschland und Frankreich – ein Vergleich, Frankfurt a.M./New York 1993

sory, control and preparatory levels, because relatively unqualified labour is used at the bottom level whose work is highly tailored or rationalised.

Within the context of German labour organisation these numerous supervisory levels are not necessary because the skilled worker is defined by the fact that he is in a position to perform complex work operations relatively independently. We are of the opinion that this organisation of labour is an important pillar of the German export industry which is after all largely based on the export of capital goods. However, these (plant engineering, machine tool manufacture, large electrical appliances, etc.) can actually only be produced by well-qualified skilled workers. It is certainly no coincidence that the model of German skilled worker training was developed essentially by the capital goods industry of the 1920s. In short: the export strength of the German economy is based not least on the existence of the social figure of the skilled worker. Whether the specific positions and works assignments of the skilled worker can in future be performed by ''side entrants'' is doubtful, these doubts relating to both the quantitative aspect of the question and the qualitative aspect. However, it is certain that the withdrawal of industry from the dual system, should it happen for reasons of cost, is based on a simple miscalculation[205].

The second argument is a pedagogic-didactic one: we are of the opinion that the majority of our youth is neither able nor willing to accept the theoretical-abstract learning structure of the grammar school with its remoteness from practice and life. The social opening up of the grammar school has not yet resulted in its curriculum and forms of learning being substantially changed with a view to the new clientele which it already has to serve. Both teachers and pupils are suffering from this. Despite some attempts to bring ''practical learning'' into grammar schools, so far only the vocational training system is able to offer this type of learning to the majority of our youth.

This objection is aimed at precisely the cardinal weakness of the ''meritocratic principle''. Burkart Lutz has briefly and clearly outlined the risks of unrestricted implementation of this educational and socio-political strategy: Lutz claims that this development could end in a situation ''in which

---

205 Cf. Bardeleben, R. v. et al: Kosten und Nutzen der betrieblichen Berufsausbildung, in: Berufsbildung in Wissenschaft und Praxis 23 (1994), p. 3-12

the skill of working on one's own responsibility and of mastering technology independently as a matter of course as ... required of as much of the workforce as possible by the trend in needs is acquired only by a small number of the youth at the highest level of a highly hierarchical, highly selective training system, e.g. at engineering universities, in the natural science faculties of high-ranking universities or in the medical schools. In these circumstances the majority of the new blood would be characterised by their failure in the competition for access to the higher training and education courses, whilst they could obtain vocational qualifications only in the form of the scholastic imparting of abstract knowledge, which as such secures no practical mastery of an (even very narrow) vocational field''[206].

So does the dual system of vocational training in Germany have a future, or is this all behind it? In our opinion nobody can make a reliable forecast at present of the survival chances of this qualificationsystem in Germany. However, the first thing which will change under the pressure of global competitive forces and technical-organisational responsibilities is undoubtedly vocational training, or more precisely, its industrial variant. As Burkart Lenz, a proven expert on international employment and training structures, says: ''We have come to a dead end as far as industrial worker qualification is concerned.'' Neither can strong signs of new movements be made out in this area in other comparable industrial countries[207].

Vocational training will therefore change; whether in the direction of stabilisation or dissolution of the dual system cannot be prophesied with the desired certainty at present. Vocational training will certainly change because in addition to the economically induced forces of modern industrial societies of the western type, a new ''social figure'' of employee is taking shape. He is characterised by greater self-awareness, more precise ideas about his future career, by his making greater reference to his own emotionality and personality development and the desire for time allocation appropriate to his needs at work. Company or waged work will thus be confronted with higher demands in respect of both the activity profile and the rights of co-determination in company processes[208].

---

206 Cf. Lutz, B.: Herausforderungen an eine zukunftsorientierte Berufsbildungspolitik, in: Bundesinstitut für Berufsbildung (Publisher): Die Rolle der beruflichen Bildung und Berufsbildungsforschung im internationalen Vergleich, Berlin/Bonn 1991, 27-36, p. 33
207 Cf. Lutz, B.: Welche Zukunft haben die Facharbeiter?, in: Berufsbildung, Nr. 2/1992, 3-7, p. 6

This new "activity type" is already represented by the younger generation of employees in the services sector; its role as a model for industrial workers and other groups of employees is unquestionable, as numerous studies demonstrate. The structural changes mentioned above in employment and the changed training behaviour of the upcoming generation will favour it spreading out further.

The traditional compulsory vocational school has also lost the justification for its existence in view of these radical processes of change. The two major central orientation variables of its training work have already largely evaporated:

1. The traditional clientele of the vocational school – the capable lower school leavers: "the best sons of the people" – no longer exists. The good third of those leaving this school who are still found in the dual system covers fairly precisely the proportion of the losers in the general education competition. Vocational training, particularly in the restructured training vocations, is asking too much of them. For this reason the vocational school population currently exists of 60 % young adults with intermediate and higher school qualifications whose specific training needs are simply ignored by the traditional vocational school curriculum.
2. The emphasis of the traditional training job of the vocational school – imparting technical theory – is noticeably evaporating. "The ... distribution of tasks between vocational school and company, according to which practical qualification takes place in the company and theoretical training is given primarily in the vocational school, can no longer be maintained"[209].

Since the first speculative restructuring procedures for trainingvocations in the 1980s we can see a clear tendency towards "the incorporation of vocational training" (Georg). The increasing theoretical and extra-functional loading of the vocational qualification has not strengthened the vocational school as a place of learning; on the contrary, the necessity of organising

---

208 Cf. e.g. Baethge, M.: Arbeit, Vergesellschaftung, Identität. Zur zunehmenden Subjektivierung der Arbeit, in: Zapf, W. (Publisher): Die Modernisierung moderner Gesellschaften, Frankfurt a.M. 1991, p. 260 ff.
209 Cf. Arnold, R.: Das duale System der Berufsausbildung hat eine Zukunft, in: Leviathan (1993), 89-97, p. 96

vocational learning in complex learning processes associated with the learning aim of "vocational capacity to act" has devalued the traditional learning programme of the vocational school drastically. Almost all advanced learning procedures of vocational training which have been developed in recent years originate from the corporate environment.

In a historical perspective the existence of the vocational school today is equivalent to the further training school of the 1890s and one is almost inclined to apply the harsh verdict of Georg Kerschensteiner concerning the general further training school to the vocational school today: "... the students are indifferent, the companies troublesome, the teachers perform a vain labour of love"[210]. The classical compulsory vocational school, we could exaggerate, is only held together by the duty to attend school; its organisational and pedagogic concept is obsolete.

The possible total loss of function of the vocational school as a place of learning would however not automatically bring about the end of the dual system. Its duality is in no way based upon a singular institutional arrangement – company and vocational school as places of learning – but on the tension between its two "functional elements", a private training market and state vocational training legislation. Within this context other institutional variants more open to the future are conceivable. To date there has been a lack of ideas pointing the way to the future as well as a lack of political commitment to the initiation of such a process of renewal of the dual system.

---

210 The original quote has been altered slightly; rather than "the companies", at that time the quote referred to "the master craftsmen".